LOUISA MAY ALCOTT

LOUISA MAY ALCOTT

from a photograph made in 1876

LOUISA MAY

ALCOTT

BY

KATHARINE ANTHONY

GREENWOOD PRESS, PUBLISHERS
WESTPORT, CONNECTICUT

HOUSTON PUBLIC LIBRARY

Library of Congress Cataloging in Publication Data

Anthony, Katharine Susan, 1877-1965.
  Louisa May Alcott.

  Reprint of the 1st ed. published by Knopf,
New York.
  Bibliography: p.
  Includes index.
    1. Alcott, Louisa May, 1832-1888--Biography.
2. Novelists, American--19th century--Biography.
[PS1018.A7 1977]   813'.4   77-2388
ISBN 0-8371-9552-7

Copyright renewed 1965 by Aida Anthony Wheadon.

Originally published in 1938 by Alfred A. Knopf, New York

Reprinted with the permission of Aida Anthony Wheadon

Reprinted in 1977 by Greenwood Press, Inc.

Library of Congress catalog card number 77-2388

ISBN 0-8371-9552-7

Printed in the United States of America

TO

Alice Mary Kimball

PREFACE

It has been my observation that all books written about the subject of this biography, whatever their nature and purpose, are classed as children's books. The following life of Louisa May Alcott, it may therefore be stated here, was not written for children. However great her interest in and identification with children, her life was a subject for consideration by adult intelligences and as such and for such it is here presented. I sincerely hope that the volume will not take the unfailing path to the children's department which seems to await all books on this subject.

Louisa May Alcott was a woman of more significance than is usually accorded her. The inheritor and disseminator of ideas which have had much to do with the making of our country, she has always been an important social influence. Because of her never-failing imprint on the young as a story-teller, she has kept alive the spirit and the ideals of the age to which she belonged. Claimed as a Victorian,

Louisa Alcott merited this appellation only to a degree. She was born too soon to escape the marks of an earlier and more heroic time.

The following biography is also the biography of her family. The Alcotts were a curiously rich vein of outcropping talent. Great as was Louisa's share of the family gift, one or two of her sisters might have attained equal distinction had they possessed the same ambition. The father was a famous man in his own right and the mother was a disappointed careerist. Common talent added to intense family emotion made the Alcotts a solid unit, so that the story of one of them cannot be told without the stories of all the others.

In the course of the three years spent on it, this study has been aided by sources impossible to enumerate or describe here. But the writings of Cornelia Meigs, Honoré Willsie Morrow, and Lucile Gulliver constitute a debt which must be mentioned. Persons who met Louisa Alcott in her later years have generously supplied their reminiscences. Descendants of the family have patiently submitted to questions and requests. The publishers of Louisa May Alcott's works have kindly delved into their archives. Personal friends of the author have given valuable time to the pursuit of successful clues and the elimination of mare's nests.

PREFACE

A wide and varied correspondence has netted many strategic and valued hints. To the two who originally suggested this unexpectedly difficult but enjoyable enterprise, Blanche Knopf and Thomas Beer, this book is most of all indebted. The principal literary sources will be found in the bibliography. The writer alone is responsible for the selection and arrangement of facts and events and for the underlying interpretation.

K. A.

CONTENTS

xi

ILLUSTRATIONS

LOUISA MAY ALCOTT

CHAPTER I

The Birthday

One Saturday afternoon in Boston in the late summer of 1828 a man and a woman were sitting together in a comfortably furnished parlour. The woman had a pair of fine hazel eyes and a rather broad determined face. The man was a tall blond, with a long face and blue, ecstatic eyes. The woman wore wide crinoline skirts underneath a full-busted waist, and the man a white stock that came up to his chin, a long-tailed coat, and very tight trousers. Neither was exactly in the first flush of youth, but they were evidently engaged in an ardent romance.

The man had reached the age of twenty-nine and the woman twenty-eight. He was reading aloud from a magazine, and she was listening attentively. The magazine from which the man was reading was called the

Journal of Education, and the voice that read was charming and mellow. When the man with the charming voice had read all the way through one article he began on another and read straight through that. The woman's attention remained flatteringly unrelaxed. The man read on, musically intoning " Hints for the Improvement of Early Education and Nursery Discipline " and " Instructions for the Early Management of Children with a View to their Future Character." The Puritan lovers passed several Saturday afternoon hours in this way.

When they had finished the magazines, the couple turned to the man's personal diary. But now they moved over to the sofa and sat side by side reading the finely written pages. It was not a gay history — this diary of a Connecticut schoolmaster — but as the couple on the sofa read they became quite merry. In the discreet white-curtained parlour their laughter rang out again and again quite cheerily.

2

Amos Bronson Alcott, the reader of that afternoon, and Abigail May, his companion, had known each other for about a year. Their friendship had developed chiefly through correspondence, for Alcott had but recently come to live in Boston. But the correspondence had been industrious, as Abigail May was nothing if not a letter-writer. " It is my impression," says Honoré Willsie Morrow, " that Abba was a bit forward in urging the young schoolmaster to write often." At the beginning of their acquaintance Abba's firm hand drew and tied together the strands of their common destiny.

" Looked over my friend's journal with him," wrote she briefly in her own diary that evening. " We had a most facetious interview."

A few weeks later the serious-minded suitor was presented to Colonel Joseph May, Abigail's father. It was the beginning of a tacit if not formal engagement. The visit took place on Sunday. " At Colonel May's," wrote the enraptured Alcott. " With the family of this benevolent man I was already acquainted, with Samuel Joseph May of Brooklyn, and Mrs. Samuel Greele of Boston. . . . This family is distinguished for urbanity and benevolence, for native manners and nobleness of soul, for moral purity and general beneficence." If Alcott could only have held to this high idealization of Abba's family, his prospects for a happy marriage would have been brighter. But the glamour faded all too soon. When he was presented to Abba's great-aunt, the dowager Madam Scott, who had formerly been married to Governor Hancock, his rapture utterly failed him. " She seems to be a lady of very little force of mind . . ." he wrote, " depending upon the idea of her connection with Mr. Hancock as the basis of her fame and greatness." Great-aunt Scott set the seal and stamp on his engagement to Abba by inviting the couple to dine with her on Sunday.

Alcott continued to be as much enamoured of his

Abba as ever. Abba told him a great deal about her mother, who had died, and Alcott wrote in his diary: " I can in some degree realize the character of this good woman from her influence on her children. It was this influence which made our Abba the affectionate friend, the disinterested companion, the ardent lover." One somehow fears, with Mrs. Morrow, that Abba was a bit forward in this relationship.

And yet, despite this indication of the state of things between them, for two years more they did not marry. It was a long engagement. They were Puritans and intellectuals and ambitious beings, and Alcott was poor and without prospects.

3

Abigail May was the descendant of famous ancestors. The Sewalls, her mother's family, were among the original dozen or so prominent old clans of Boston. Judge Samuel Sewall, who condemned the witches to be hung —

> ". . . the Judge of the old Theocracy,
> Whom even his errors glorified " —

was one of her progenitors. The Mays, her father's clan, also belonged to the fine folk of the old city. Her father, Colonel Joseph May, was a warden of King's Chapel for years and married as his second wife the widow of the King's Chapel rector. Abba, the step-daughter of this lady, was related by ties of blood or marriage to the best established families of Boston. She was a genuine member of its Puritan aristocracy.

Miss May, as Abba was generally called at the time when she met Alcott, was, in spite of her high birth, in a rather subordinate social position. When her father married the second time, she had left his home — in a temper, one surmises — and her life was henceforth an interminable round of visits to friends and relations. Having no independent means of subsistence and still by tradition and habits a lady, she had difficulty in maintaining herself in the state to which she had been called. This perhaps made her all the more eager to assert the gentility which should have been unquestioned.

Miss May had been from childhood in a low state of health. In this respect she claimed she was like her mother. But her buxom looks and the energy for which she was universally praised by her friends and contemporaries would indicate that her constitution was not so very feeble. Abba's mother had borne twelve children and had lived until the youngest was twenty-five, so it hardly seems as if she could have been excessively frail either. What Abba really had was the tender and easily snapped nerves of those who have too much ancestry. Everyone has ancestry, and forgets it, but behind Abba there were too many unforgotten generations — always a great burden on the last of the series.

She had little formal education. " My schooling was interrupted by ill-health," she said. She had some advanced tutoring with a friend, but it was not much. In an age when blue-stockings were common, she did not become one. Her ambition was to be an artist. She had been taught to play the piano and sang well. Her literary taste had been formed by her father, to whom she read, " while he shaved each morning," from the works of Dr. Samuel Johnson. This habit had given her the very excellent Johnsonian style that she used in her letters. Style is not acquired without striving; so Abba was evidently not without literary ambition.

In the spring of 1828 Abba May was approaching the age of twenty-eight. No longer verdantly young, she was more or less on the minds of a large connection of relatives and friends. Some of them were on the board of a little charity school and they asked Abba to be on the board and to become the teacher of the school. This she immediately saw as an opportunity for Bronson Alcott, in whom she was much interested, to come to Boston. " There is in this great flock," she wrote him, " a little wee lamb that I wish to have nourished . . . an infant school for the very poor children. . . . I wish that you were in Boston, that you might aid the good work." Alcott responded that he would come, all the more since Abba May was to be his assistant in the school. But by the time Bronson had reached Boston, Abba had given up the idea of being an assistant teacher, owing to her poor health. Alcott was intensely disappointed. Abba resigned sadly and found a substitute to take her place, a maiden lady who was somewhere on the farther side of forty.

MRS. JOHN HANCOCK (MADAM SCOTT)

from a miniature in the Arthur C. Nash Collection

So she remained the rather magnificent Miss Abba May, talented and distinguished, but wandering and unsettled withal.

4

Amos Bronson Alcott was born on November 29, 1799 on a farm at Spindle Hill, near Wolcott, Connecticut, a small village about twenty miles north of New Haven. On this farm three generations of Alcotts had lived and died before him. He had as many unforgotten ancestors as Abba; but they belonged to a rather crude civilization, the men of the district where he was born being half artisans and half farmers. Alcott's father was such a man; he was a carpenter-farmer. He had taken a wife of more cultivation than himself, Alcott's mother being fairly educated and having a brother who was an Episcopal clergyman in Cheshire. Alcott's mother was determined that her eldest son should follow in the exalted footsteps of his uncle.

But the times and the locality were against her. Alcott's father put the boy to work in a clock-factory about two miles from home. Here Bronson easily made connections with the pedlars who came to the factory to replace their stock. Bronson joined the migrators, who regularly went south in the fall and returned in the spring, and spent four or five successive winters wandering through Maryland, Virginia, and the Carolinas. He was sometimes with a companion, sometimes alone. A planter invited him to remain as a guest and use his well-stocked library, which Alcott, to the detriment of his pedlar's trade but the improvement of his mind, accordingly did. A colony of Quakers took him in when he was ill and nursed him. Once he was robbed and beaten. All these adventures made deep marks on his life and character and left romantic memories. It would be interesting to know how near Alcott came to Washington; but, as pedlars usually kept to the back-country districts, it was probably not very near. He must have fallen in with Jeffersonian ideas, however, for he came out of his *Wanderjahre* with all his radical tendencies strengthened.

Alcott had thought of teaching in Virginia, where so many New England young men taught in those days, but he had not succeeded in finding a position. On his return he began teaching in the district school near his home. Rotating from school to school as country schoolteachers usually did, he came at last to the town of Cheshire, the home of his distinguished uncle in whose footsteps his mother had expected him to follow. Alcott decided that he owed it to this town to do his best and introduced his own type of school, which, whether he followed Pestalozzi and Froebel or merely his own ideas, meant radical innovations. But the townspeople did not like his innovations, and the outcome, sadly forecast by this note in Alcott's journal: " Those dissatisfied with our plans have engaged an instructor and commenced another school this day with fifteen pupils," was that Alcott's school was closed.

Alcott had waged a brisk war with his detractors, however, and in the course of it had made a name for himself among the reformers of his state. He had kept his standing also among the conventional educators. He taught school in Connecticut for another whole year, having been recalled after the period in Cheshire by the village of Bristol, where he had taught school previously. If his professional life had not become involved with his emotional affairs, he might have remained in his native state and pursued his calling quite successfully. It was a chance meeting with Miss Abigail May at the home of her brother, the Reverend Samuel J. May, in Brooklyn, Connecticut, that changed the course of his fortunes.

5

To Amos Bronson Alcott, fresh from the simplicities of Connecticut, a real Bostonian young lady seemed like the epitome of culture. As Abba played and sang to him in Mrs. Samuel Greele's parlour, she seemed no less than one of the world's prima donnas. He had a great respect for intellect and character. " I know of no young lady equally intelligent on the subject of infant education," he wrote intensely, " and no one feeling a deeper interest in the welfare of the young." Abba had all the graces; she was gifted, charming, and humane.

To Abba May, Alcott was that priceless boon to a genteel but poor young woman — a suitor. She admired Alcott also. His ability as a writer commanded her respect. For Alcott could write well in those early days. A little pamphlet by him entitled: *Observations on the Principles and Methods of Infant Instruction,* and signed: " A. B. Alcott, Teacher of an Elementary School," survives to show that Alcott had a direct, clear essay style. His reputation as an author aroused Abba's pride in him, and her love was sustained by it.

But, though their relation depended on other things, both of them were in love. Their belated passions were aroused. Puritan lovers that they were and late drinkers at the deep stream of life, they entered upon their experience with all the force of emotions released after having been long dammed up.

And yet they delayed marriage. Two winters passed over the engaged couple, while they remained separated; for Abba, by the force of circumstances, had been obliged to go to Brooklyn, Connecticut, when Alcott came to Boston. Mrs. Samuel Greele, her sister, died, and Abba had to go away to the home of her brother. From a distance of a hundred miles she watched her lover's career develop in the city while she lived in a small provincial village. From this point of view she saw that, while Alcott prospered in other ways, he still did not prosper financially. So the correspondence in which they both excelled was carried on indefinitely.

And then, without any outward change in their circumstances, Abba went up to Boston and they were married. The ceremony was performed quietly but impressively in King's Chapel, on May 23, 1830. It was a union of romantics and intellectuals. Alcott had only a pittance for a salary and Abba's only portion was household furniture. But in aspirations they were rich. " Our lives shall be spent in the mutual elevation and advancement of each other," wrote Alcott to Abba concerning their future. In regard to the simplest facts of life — the coming of children, the responsibility of family life, its foundation in economics — they were both as unsuspecting infants.

6

But Alcott's writings in the *Journal of Education* and other periodicals as well had made his school famous. Situated in the heart of the city, it was sought out by many visitors, and the fame was very gratifying to the director. Some of the visitors came from a long distance. One day a grey-clad, broad-hatted figure, whom Alcott recognized at once for a Quaker, a sect which he had learned to know in the South, came into the school. He had travelled all the way from Philadelphia to see Alcott's classes.

The visitor was a prosperous farmer. He lived outside Philadelphia on a large estate with a correspondingly large house in which he was bringing up seven children. He had read Alcott's writings and sensed in him from afar a kindred soul and the man he thought he would like to have educate his children. The two became friends at their first meeting. To a similarity in

13

views and outlook was added a common taste in hob-
bies; they met as if they had known each other always.

Allowing for this strong affinity, the result of Reuben
Haines's visit was rather precipitate and unexpected.
He proposed that Alcott should close his Boston school
and move to Germantown, Pennsylvania, at once. Alcott agreed to do this. Giving scant notice to his pupils
and taking with him a wife who was expecting a child
soon, he prepared immediately to migrate. In less than
a month the Alcotts were on a steamer in the Atlantic
headed for Philadelphia.

A more prudent person would have looked ahead
more carefully. Alcott was to have a house free of rent
to live in and to keep his school in. The seven Haines
children were to go to his school, and their tuition was
the foundation of its support. He was supposed to build
up the rest of the school from the environment. But in
a rural community like Germantown there was but a
thin population to draw upon, and the population, except Haines, was not well-to-do. As a matter of fact,
Haines eventually paid the tuition of most of the other
children as well as of his own. Everything came as a
benefit from him, the local squire and patriarch.

Innocent egoist that she was, Abba also asked no
questions; she was chiefly concerned to convince her
father in Boston that the change represented a great
upward step in their fortunes. How she must have ab-
horred the muddy streets and simple houses of the
crude German village! But Abba said nothing of such

things in her letters to Boston; she wrote glowing accounts of everything back home. The house they lived in — a very good house, it is true, called Pine Place — she referred to as a " Little Paradise." Conditions were in truth promising for the first year or two.

Then the sponsor died. This was in the spring of 1832. The hale, hearty man disappeared one day from the scene as if he had never existed and his protection of the Alcotts was as if it had never been. They did not know at first how great was their loss, so little observant were they of practical things in general. They tried to carry on by taking boarding pupils. When this did not work, they moved to Philadelphia, thinking that after all a school in the city might do better. But Philadelphia proved indifferent to Alcott's educational theories. The family were finally stranded, like barnstorming actors. There was nothing left for them to do but go back to Boston and open there again the school they had with so little thought abandoned.

So, after rather more than three years of absence, they returned with empty pockets and deflated reputation. Alcott was cheerfully ready, if he must, to begin again at the bottom. But Abba was far from cheerful.

7

They brought with them two children. The children had both been born in Germantown, at Pine Place, in the same upstairs bedroom. Their names were Anna Bronson Alcott and Louisa May Alcott.

When, on a certain wintry night around Thanksgiving 1832, Abba Alcott lay abed expecting the birth of her second infant, naturally both she and her husband very much wanted it to be a boy. The wish was intensified by the thought that if the child was born, as it probably would be, on November 29, it would have the same birthday as its father. The coming baby, as if in response to that wish, arrived just half an hour after midnight, on the auspicious day. But it was a girl.

The 29th of November was a very special date in Alcott's mind. It was not only his birthday; it was also Columbus's. He treasured the coincidence. He and Columbus shared it now with a third important person. Alcott wrote in his diary: " A daughter was born on . . . my birthday, being 33 years of age. This is a most interesting event."

The child was named for Abba's sister who had died, Mrs. Samuel Greele of Boston. " Abba inclines to call the babe *Louisa May,*" wrote Alcott to Abba's father in Boston, " a name to her full of every association connected with amiable benevolence and excellent worth. I hope *its present possessor* may rise to equal attainment and deserve a place in the estimation of Society." Alcott already nourished aspirations for his daughter Louisa — aspirations which were in a way a historic prophecy.

When Louisa was a month old, someone who saw her said: " It is the prettiest, best little thing in the world. You will wonder to have me call anything so young

16

pretty, but it is really so in an uncommon degree: it has a fair complexion, dark bright eyes, long dark hair, a high forehead, and altogether a countenance of more than usual intelligence." This description of the baby in her cradle might have been used later of the girl in her teens. Louisa kept her bright eyes, fine hair, and good features, though her fair baby skin was replaced by an olive complexion.

Her birth unfortunately fell in the anxious period that followed the death of Reuben Haines. The gates of the " Little Paradise " had closed on the distressed Alcotts. The spirit of peace and plenty, which for more than a year had presided over the household, had fled. While Louisa lay and looked at the ceiling with her dark bright eyes, her parents' world was crumbling around them. As she cooed and gurgled her way toward the maturity of one year, the foundations of their lives tottered and trembled. The universe was kept in place transiently by props, but the time came when the last feeble stay went down. An atmosphere of despair and flight succeeded. Pine Place, " Little Paradise," was deserted.

Louisa's home was exchanged for one in Philadelphia; or, rather, the familiar floor on which she crept about exploringly was exchanged for another floor. And still the universe about her rocked and swayed and trembled. The air was filled with the tones of her mother's voice raised in anger; and it was painfully oppressive with her father's silence afterwards.

And then, the universe all at once settled in its moorings again. Louisa found herself moving in her mother's arms while her sister rode high in her father's. They were all going somewhere together.

The tall man and the firm-looking woman, each with a child in arms, walked on the boat that was headed for Boston.

CHAPTER II

Mother and Daughter

THE VOYAGE from Philadelphia to Boston was a long one in 1834, even though it was made by steamships. Alcott was returning to Boston to pick up the threads dropped almost four years ago. It was another venture into the unknown; after so long an absence old friends might have forgotten him. But Dr. William Henry Channing, the great Unitarian leader, had promised his support, and the Reverend Samuel Joseph May, Abba's brother and staunch friend, had also promised to stand by. And Alcott was easily encouraged. Abba too was almost hopeful. They had survived a crisis, and friends had rallied to their support. And she was at least going to see Boston again. Their furniture safely stowed away in the hold of the ship, they settled themselves for a long, uneventful journey.

The summer days passed peacefully. The ship ploughed smoothly through the calm ocean. Then one day the younger Alcott baby, Louisa, a year and a half old, could not be found. A search was made on all the decks and through all the staterooms, but nowhere was the missing little one discovered. Consternation reigned supreme. At last in the engine-room, whither her unusually active little body had propelled itself, the baby turned up. Her frock was covered with engine-grease and coal-dust and she was happily absorbed in watching the machinery. A year and a half old, the run-away had had the thrilling taste of being the cause of surrounding excitement. The boat-trip was made memorable for the family by Louisa's escapade.

Arriving in Boston, they landed at a wharf in Front Street and moved into a house only a stone's throw away. Louisa's first home in Boston was associated with the smell of sea-water and salt spray.

2

The schoolmaster spent much time in the care of his own children. Abba Alcott was not a nose-wiping mother. Her dislike of teaching was frankly based on the fact that she had neither the temperament nor the patience required for it. With her own children she was the same. Let sickness or accident or any crisis befall them and Abba rose at once to the worst emergency; but in the common, everyday, unheroic tasks of the nursery she was not interested. As she said of the occasions when she tried teaching children, " I love their society when I can unreservedly communicate and associate with them. I love to teach when I can do it in my own way." Her motherhood was equally temperamental. Alcott on the contrary was not only patient but very skilful with babies. He wrote a book for mothers, full of practical advice and suggestions, but it was never published, owing to Emerson's fear that it would make his friend ridiculous.

Alcott was no mere nursemaid, however; he was a child-psychologist. He was the first parent in the field to make a scientific study of his descendants. The two Alcott children early proved that an infant can be made the object of psychological research without injury to its development. Alcott had written almost a volume about his elder daughter before she was five months old. He followed it with a similar but less exhaustive study of Louisa. In that sentimental age and on the most sentimental of all subjects, parenthood, he strove — not always successfully, it is true — to be scientific.

While Louisa was still living in the little house in Front Street, sniffing the smell of wharves and sea-air and running about tirelessly on her first little legs, Alcott wrote this elaborate analysis of her character:

" Louisa is a guideless creature, the child of instinct yet unenlightened by love. On the impetuous stream of instinct she has set sail and regardless alike of the quick-sand and the rocks, of the careering winds and winter currents that oppose the course, she looks only toward the objects of her desire and steers proudly, adventurously, and yet without compass or chart save the gale and gleaming stars of her own will, toward the heaven of her hopes. The stronger the opposing gale, the more sullenly and obstinately does she ply her energies and when compelled to yield, she yields but to await the calming of the angry waters that she may ride on again toward her end. Richly freighted and heavyladen is her spirit but it plays too safely with the lifting waves and exults in its own unbridled strength; uncurbed, untaught, unguided by the skill of this life's voyagers. Experience will teach her in due time, if she have the true helmsman to guide and protect her, the secret of her strength and the way to avail herself of its potency."

The little Alcott girls, owing to their father's curious method of observing and reporting them, were by way of becoming rather famous characters in their tender years. People began calling them model children and prodigies, and the appellations stuck. The Alcotts were among the most talked-of folk in Boston.

3

One unexplained circumstance of Louisa's childhood is that she did not attend her father's school. Anna, her older sister, was a pupil from the age of three, for this was the age at which Alcott started children. But Louisa reached the age of six without having been enrolled. The omission, combined with Abba Alcott's distaste for child-minding, may account for little Louisa's rather eventful life in the city.

She roamed about somewhat freely for one of her tender age. " The Alcotts allowed their children so much freedom," says one biographer, " that some of their friends thought sufficient care was not taken in regard to their associates. . . . In reply to a question upon that subject Mrs. Alcott replied, ' I can trust my daughters, and this is the best way to teach them how to shun these sins and comfort these sorrows.' " Mrs. Alcott began her system early. Sometimes the wandering infant met her grandfather, Colonel Joseph May, in the street, and the elderly gentleman, who is said to have been the original of " The Last Leaf," took her into a shop and bought her a card of gingerbread. But not all of her adventures were so pleasant. Once she fell into the Frog Pond on the Common and might have been drowned but for the prompt action of a coloured boy who pulled her out. No one ever knew the name of the coloured boy, but he became a legendary hero in the family.

More memorable was the occasion when she was lost. Coming home late from the Common one afternoon, she was unable to find her way, perhaps because the family had recently moved, for it was about that time that they went from Front Street to Cottage Place. The bewildered infant sank down in a convenient doorway where a big dog lay at rest; snuggling up to the animal, she went to sleep by his side. At nine o'clock she was awakened by the loud voice of the town-crier —

who must have looked remarkably like her grand-father — loudly proclaiming the loss of " a little girl, six years old, in a pink frock, white hat, and new green shoes." Louisa recognized herself at once and called out blithely from the doorway: " Why, dat's me." The town-crier took her home and fed her before restoring her to her anxious parents.

Louisa was becoming too adept at being lost and found. This escapade of hers called for action — so her mother thought. Descendant of the Puritans, with the blood of Judge Sewall in her veins, Abba promptly put the criminal in the stocks. Louisa was tied publicly to the sofa and left there to do penance. The culprit felt thoroughly disgraced and shamefully punished. Running away was always afterwards associated in her mind with the idea of crime. Whenever she *did* run away, as frequently happened, she felt like a criminal.

At the age of six Louisa's active, muscular strength began to assert itself. She could run, jump, and wrestle as few children of that age could. She could drive her hoop without stopping all the way around the Common. The boys on the Common stopped playing football to watch her do it. Louisa would have preferred to play football with them, but the next best thing was to distract their attention from the game with her hoop-rolling.

Another vigorous sport she liked was a kind of roller-coasting. Near Cottage Place was a piano-factory to which Louisa sometimes repaired with a boy companion. Their favourite game consisted in climbing into one of the heavy trucks left standing about, and riding down an inclined plane till the truck stopped with a thunderous crash at the bottom. Fortunately, they enjoyed this sport to their heart's content without an accident's happening.

When Louisa was seven years old, her mother gave her a doll. " My dear little girl," she said in the note accompanying it, " Will you accept this doll from me on your seventh birthday? She will be a quiet playmate for my active Louisa for seven years more. Be a kind mamma and love her for my sake." But the doll was too late to compete with the wild free life on the Common, with the long days on vacant lots where she played with tenement children until she forgot to go home for lunch, and with the companionship of boys as active and vigorous as herself. The taste for adventure had already developed in Louisa and it was perhaps already too strong ever to be eradicated. Her chief interest in the doll was to make bonnets for it, which she adorned with feathers pulled out of the rooster's tail, the bird having first been chased to a glorious finish.

But the rooster and doll-bonnets came after the family had moved from Boston to Concord.

4

Bronson Alcott reopened his school in the Masonic Temple in Tremont Street, next door to King's Chapel. It was an unusually elegant school. He made the place beautiful, " sparing no expense," he said, " to surround the senses with appropriate emblems of intellectual and spiritual life." Busts of the Greek philosophers, along with other statuary, were placed along the walls. (The bust of Socrates is still preserved on the dusty shelf of an old house in Concord.) His discipline was mild to a degree unheard-of in those days, though he did not absolutely eschew the birch-rod as is reported. His curriculum avoided the mechanical memorizing which was usual at the time, and instead of using the Peter Parley parrot-books he introduced original works of literature. Alcott's personality was the supreme mark of difference between his school and others, for children really liked him and talked freely to him.

Alcott's income from this school was eighteen hundred dollars a year; one hundred and fifty dollars a month. This was to his simple standards an unexampled fortune, and out of his new wealth he bought his elegant furnishings. But he had also rent to pay and his family to support. Incurable optimist that he was, he could never remember the warning early given him by his mother that " he, as well as others, was subject to disappointments." He taught his Temple school happily, making long plans for the future and never dreaming that good fortune could be precarious.

For the first time his family life and school life were separated. This was a more promising situation than had yet obtained for him. He wrote in his diary: " By the present arrangement I shall never be occupied with practical instruction more than five hours a day, and, ultimately, perhaps, not more than three. I shall be able to do better justice to my family than I have done."

His assistant in the school was Elizabeth Peabody, who afterwards introduced the kindergarten system in Boston. Miss Peabody was the teacher of the older children, and Alcott taught the younger ones. Together they ran the school to the satisfaction of the patrons and the approval of the public. Alcott's reputation rose again as it had risen before he went to Pennsylvania.

And just when the schoolmaster thought he was sailing most successfully, his ship ran on the shoals. Again he entertained a visitor. Miss Harriet Martineau, the English author, came to Boston and visited the school. On the strength of a brief half-hour in Alcott's classroom, she went home and wrote the severe criticism contained in her *Society in America*. Mistress of a harsh and vituperative style, she turned it in all its strength upon the Alcott experiment. She gave voice to a current of antipathy which had previously existed but had found no spokesman. The criticism was strengthened by Alcott's unfortunately publishing at just this time his *Conversations with Children on the Gospels*, regarded as an irreligious and obscene book. Purporting to be a verbatim report of his discussions with his pupils, it gave his enemies seemingly all the material they needed to destroy him. If this was what went on in the new school, the public was shocked. Old Puritan Boston revived its past history and set upon Alcott fiercely as a heretic.

In a short time it was apparent that the Temple School was doomed.

5

Though Louisa did not attend her father's school, he taught her at home. His teaching embraced everything, from how to sit in the little chair he bought her to how to tell good from evil. " Louisa is making rapid progress in spoken language," he noted. " She adds new words to her vocabulary daily. I believe she appreciates *all* the relations of expression, using every part of speech." Before she could read, she was aware that children's books existed. The nursery of this straitened home contained the complete works of Miss Edgeworth and Mrs. Barbauld and all the good current juvenile books. Louisa's favourite story was called *Little Woman and Peddler* — which in view of her most famous work and her father's early wanderings is an interesting infantile choice.

The little girls dramatized and acted their nursery tales. *Jack and the Beanstalk, Cinderella,* and *Pilgrim's Progress* were done over and over. When they played *Pilgrim's Progress,* Abba Alcott gave them her piece-bags to tie on their backs and sent them climbing from the cellar to the garret of the house with their burdens. This game they still played after they were well-grown girls. The habit of dramatizing everything, including, unfortunately, their own personal relations, was inherent in the family.

One day, on her third birthday, Louisa *was* taken to school. It was Alcott's birthday too — his thirty-sixth. In the graceful and beautiful surroundings of Alcott's unique schoolroom a pretty festival took place. The pupils had woven a laurel crown for the schoolmaster and a wreath of flowers for his little daughter. Louisa, in the seventh heaven, shared the honours of the day with her father. The pupils danced around them singing an ode that had been composed for the occasion:

> A time for joy, — for joy!
>   Let joy then swell around;
> From every girl and boy
>   Let joy's full tones resound.
>
> This hour in love we come,
>   With hearts of happy mirth;
> We've sallied forth from home
>   To celebrate a birth.
>
> A time for joy, — for joy!
>   Let joy then swell around;
> From every girl and boy
>   Let joy's full tones resound.

Then Louisa was allowed to distribute the refreshments. Standing on a table, she handed a cake to each of the children as they marched by. As the end of the line approached, the little hostess saw to her consternation that there were not enough cakes to go round. In a panic she clutched the last cake and refused to part with it. But her mother interfered at this juncture. " It is always better to give away than to keep the nice things," she said; " so I know my Louy will not let the little friend go without." And the lively, impetuous, and ofttimes recalcitrant child resigned the last cake to the little friend, receiving in return a kiss from her mother and public applause. It was a bitter-sweet experience for little Louisa, one which lay at the back of much that happened in her life. It was lovely to be a heroine, but then it was ofttimes as sad as it was lovely.

6

After Alcott's school failed, he could no longer live in Boston. Abba Alcott wrote to her brother early in 1840: " We go to Concord for another experiment in the art of living. . . . We have found a small cottage, with a large garden and an acre of ground for $50 a year. . . . The land Mr. Alcott thinks altogether superior to the Scituate soil; and on many accounts his local and social relations are more agreeable to him than in some regions. . . . A course of conversations has been suggested in Lexington for him. . . . Mr. Alcott hopes to get his garden tools, and to pay for transportation, from the sale of his school-room furniture, and from the articles of household use which our little house will not accommodate."

This sounded like a real escape from the heavy ex-

ABBA MAY ALCOTT

(MRS. BRONSON ALCOTT)

penses of Boston life. Still rent was rent, even if it was the minimum, and there were still human beings to be clothed, fed, and kept warm. Alcott's plan was to give lectures when he could and to earn the rest by cutting wood and mowing hay for other people in the vicinity. With an acre of ground for a garden, he felt that he and his family could live mainly out of that, especially as they were vegetarians and he was an excellent gardener. He forgot the especially hard winters of the country and the large stores required to survive them. Abba's letter to her brother continued: " The quiet, pure air, and genial influence of the approaching season may promote a more vigorous state of health; and then we cannot materially suffer, even if the patience of the most tried friendship should weary of our dependence, and love should chill by our absence." Abba's literary style never failed her even if her prophecies might.

So, on a moist day in the first week of April 1840, the Alcott family arrived in the village of Concord. With a flourish which they never seemed able to avoid making, no matter how hard-pressed, they spent the night at the Middlesex Hotel, a once proud hostelry that has long since vanished. On one side the hotel looked out on the mill-dam and on the other on the sloping elm-dotted surface of the village green. It overlooked and dominated the main part of the town. After spending the night there, they went on the next day to the cottage they had rented.

7

Though Abba had said nothing of it in her letter to her brother, the choice of Concord as a retreat was not accidental. Concord was the home of Ralph Waldo Emerson, and Emerson had suggested that Alcott should come and live there.

Emerson and Alcott had become acquainted in June 1836, when the fame of Alcott's school was at glowing heat. Emerson just walked into the schoolroom one day, as Haines had done earlier, and he and Alcott had been similarly enraptured at the sight of each other. Alcott fascinated most people who approached him nearly; and for Emerson, who was silent himself and loved fluent conversation in others, he had an especially strong attraction. After this meeting they became fast friends and saw each other every week, developing the relation of a New England Schiller and Goethe.

When the Boston Puritans attacked Alcott's school, Emerson sprang loyally to his support. Disliking controversy as he did, he nevertheless came forward with bold letters to the newspapers; while men like Richard Henry Dana, who had enjoyed the use of Alcott's premises for his lectures free of charge, and an anonymous Harvard professor, whose unsigned opinion of Alcott's book did the most damage of all, either said nothing in his defence or joined the ranks of his persecutors. While Emerson wrote letters to the newspapers, Margaret Fuller wrote a drastic rebuke to Harriet Martineau; but these two allies of Alcott's carried little weight with the old guard of the city, which now saw its chance to register its dislike of the whole group. Emerson did more than write letters; he went from door to door in Boston trying to find employment for Alcott. When this failed, he thought he had proposed a solution in the retirement to Concord to a life of manual labour combined with lecturing.

More hard times followed for the Alcotts. Bronson found that even as a wood-cutter he could not earn money. Lectures were as sparse as berries in the springtime. The social status of the family was painfully undetermined; they were not real homesteaders like the Emersons, the Pratts, and the Thoreaus, who, though they were intellectuals and transcendentalists, owned their land. Alcott was a tenant.

Abba, unfitted for domestic routine as she was, was surrounded by four children. A third daughter had been born in Boston, while the school had still been doing well, and had been named Elizabeth for Miss Elizabeth Peabody. Bronson was keeping up the tradition of naming his daughters for distinguished women. A few months after their arrival in Concord a fourth daughter was added. Even Bronson's optimism was a little shaken by the continued femininity of his line. " Providence, it seems," he wrote to his brother-in-law, " decrees to us daughters of love instead of sons of light." The child was named for her mother, Abba May; perhaps because Abba said to herself that there should be no other offspring and this was her last chance. The privations and hardships of this time might have well justified her in coming to such a decision.

In their outcast and troubled state Abba and Bronson turned from each other as comrades sometimes will, fatal as such a course is likely to be for both. Abba had never believed in Alcott's philosophy; now she actively discarded it. She herself was conventionally pious. Alcott, refusing to make concessions, hitched his wagon to a star and followed his friend Emerson. A barrier grew up between them, and the estrangement increased until it had become strained and bitter.

Emerson again came to his friend's rescue. Seeing that Alcott was deeply unhappy, he suggested the great panacea for all ills in those days — a trip to Europe. His devotion to Alcott led him to tramp up and down Boston trying to get a free passage for the trip. " I was not very successful in my application to our friends in Boston," he wrote, " in behalf of the voyage to England, — Mr. Phillips deeming himself unable to assist on account of his recent expense in building, etc., and Mr. Lewis explaining that he had no power to frank a berth, as Mr. Cunard had never permitted it." As usual the faithful Emerson's rounds on his friend's behalf ended at his own door. He put his hand in his pocket and gave Alcott five hundred dollars for the trip.

In the spring of 1842 Bronson left his family in the care of his young brother Junius, who came up from

Wolcott, Connecticut, for that purpose, and departed in high hopes for a new world.

8

Louisa, in Concord, lived her out-of-doors life in earnest. Hosmer Cottage, which the Alcotts occupied, looked over the meadows toward the Sudbury River, less than a quarter of a mile away. It was a tiny house, situated well out of the village. The surroundings were glorious. The marshes stretched along the river for miles and the fields rolled back gentle and placid. Nature, in which Bronson Alcott believed so ardently, was gracious, smiling, and beautiful. Louisa responded to it with even more enthusiasm perhaps than might have been wished.

Both the new doll and the new baby were forgotten. Leaving such girl-like things to her sister Anna, she sped to the wide-open spaces. She learned to climb trees, leap fences, and go berry-picking. Even if she was only eight or nine, so much free activity was decried in a girl. Without any hat on her head, her bright eyes beaming, and her long legs flying, she tore riotously about the countryside. " I was born with a boy's spirit under my bib and tucker," she said. Whether born with it or not, she developed it certainly at Hosmer Cottage in the summer of '42.

Her favourite companion was a boy named Cyrus, one of the large flock of young Hosmers who lived next door. He was the successor of the lost lamented companion of the piano-factory trucks. " Cy was a comrade after my own heart," she said long afterwards; " and for a summer we kept the neighbourhood in a ferment with our adventures and hair-breadth escapes. . . . He did not get into scrapes himself. . . . It was he who invited me to jump off the highest beam in the barn to be borne home on a board with a pair of sprained ankles. It was he who dared me to rub my eyes with red peppers, and then sympathizingly led me home blind and roaring with pain." Cyrus's sister afterwards added to Louisa's picture this further detail: " When the field-hands gave her tobacco, she chewed it so vigorously that she had to be carried home in a wheel-barrow. The boy who was there when it happened, who helped to get her home and afterwards told me all about it was my brother Cyrus." With Cyrus Hosmer at hand, Louisa must have found life in Concord sufficiently wild and exciting. Just the same, she always remembered the lad with kindness. To be allowed to tag along was of course for a little girl breathless happiness.

Louisa was growing into a tall straight girl. To length of limb she added strong muscles and sinews which made her a vigorous figure. She looked like one of the fleet brown deer which she saw in the Concord woods sometimes and which she imagined herself in some former state to have been. Her inner life was made up largely of the feeling of young well-strung muscles plying joyously through a long, active, unbroken outdoor day.

9

But the girl Louisa was a creature of moods. The sloping fields and the flowing river were as much a part of her inner life as her tomboy existence. The philosopher's child imagined strange things — things apart from all reality. A lyric spirit fluttered in the little breast. The wild little girl saw the beauty around her and felt it. Her heart melted to its call, and a precocious longing for it rose in her heart.

The same little girl who chewed tobacco with the field-hands sang this tender little song at the age of eight: —

To A Robin

Welcome, welcome, little stranger,
Fear no harm, and fear no danger;
We are glad to see you here,
For you sing, " sweet spring is near."

Now the white snow melts away;
Now the flowers blossom gay:
Come dear bird and build your nest,
For we love our robin best.

Abba was the first to see her daughter's growing power of expression. In her exile from old friends and her estrangement from Alcott she found a new interest in the development of Louisa. Annoyed with Alcott's obvious failure — his literary output had degenerated

37

into those cryptic " Orphic Sayings " he was then contributing to the *Dial* — she transferred her sympathy
and encouragement to this other aspiring author in her
family. When Louisa wrote her poem " To A Robin,"
it was her mother who expressed the greatest enthusiasm for it and made it into a historical feat. " You will
grow up a Shakespeare," said Abba, and Louisa remembered the words as if they had been laid on her
as a mission and accolade.

It was Abba also who penned this further little note
to Louisa on her tenth birthday: " I give you the pencil
case I promised, for I have observed that you are fond
of writing and wish to encourage the habit." The child
who had given away her one and only cake at the behest
of this same siren voice could not fail to respond to its
renewed magic. Louisa was at ten definitely stimulated by her mother to write. Completely out of sympathy with her husband's transcendentalism and its literary expression in the organ known as the *Dial*, Abba
registered her disapproval of that, too, in promoting
the simple but classic art of literature as practised by
her daughter. The ardent, hoydenish, dreamy Louisa
was put thoroughly out of the reach of the literary influence of the author of the " Orphic Sayings."

Another motive entered the girl's life at this time,
coming from the same maternal source. Her mother
made her a present of a small print showing a mother
and daughter together — a scene Louisa invested with
great emotional significance. The note which accom-

panied the present read: " I enclose a picture for you which I always liked very much, for I imagined that you might be just such an industrious daughter and I such a feeble but loving mother, looking to your labor for my daily bread." Louisa pasted the picture and the note in her journal and kept them there always as a steady reminder to herself of her high destiny.

CHAPTER III

Green Fruit

THE WINTER of 1842–3 brought a momentous change in the Alcott household. It was suddenly and unexpectedly increased by the advent of three strangers. The strangers came from England and their names were Charles Lane, William Lane — Charles Lane's young son — and Henry Wright. Though they dropped from the sky on the doorstep of Hosmer Cottage, it was expanded to receive them. The three visitors lived with the Alcotts all winter.

Their arrival was the fruit of Bronson Alcott's trip to England. While in England, Alcott had paid visits, in particular to Emerson's great friend, Carlyle, and to a group of his admirers who had named a school for him. The leader of the school had died while Alcott was on his way, and he found on his arrival there a peculiar situation. Alcott House, as the place was called, was in the midst of changes. The appearance of the great inspiration at this moment caused him to be involved in them. Alcott was invited to stay at Alcott House permanently, and he considered doing so. With Charles Lane, the new director of the school, he planned a socialist colony, but whether it was to be developed in England or in America was at first undetermined. Alcott's idealism was at white heat. He was no longer an outcast, but a man with a following, a prophet, and a teacher. The final decision was to come back to America.

In September 1842, therefore, Bronson Alcott, bringing Charles Lane and the others with him, arrived in Concord.

Emerson was if possible more staggered than Abba by this unexpected outcome of Alcott's trip abroad. But he met the English guests with his usual cordiality, welcoming them to the Concord circle, listening to their theories, and giving their writings a place in the *Dial,* the trancendentalist magazine of which he was editor. Here his advances stopped. He did not enter actively into the plans for the new colony.

It was a hectic winter at Hosmer Cottage. Plans and yet more plans were drafted. The projected colony, to be called the New Eden, was constantly under discussion. Theories of the good life which was to be lived there formed the staple of conversation. Principles and opinions filled the air. These were socialistic and anti-slavery in the main, but there were many side-issues.

The Hosmer Cottage residents, somewhat shut off from the world, tended to push their theories to the extreme and also to put them into practice.

That was the winter when Bronson Alcott almost went to prison for refusing to pay his taxes. There was a movement among the anti-slavery people in this direction, as a protest against the government's position on the slavery question. In Concord, Alcott and some others joined it. Alcott was arrested, but at the very door of the prison he was removed by Judge Hoar, who paid the bill for him and cleared off his debt. Alcott, nevertheless, had been in the custody of the sheriff. It was a fact that was well known and much discussed in and beyond the village that winter.

The event made Alcott and his friends more than ever determined to retire from the world. In their self-supporting colony, the New Eden, alone could they be free.

2

For the first time there was a boy in the Alcott household. Charles Lane's son, William, was about the right age to be an older brother to the Alcott girls. According to Louisa, he was " bigger than Anna," though she said nothing else about his looks at this time. The boy had no mother, so that the girls' mother stood in this relation to him. He was a totally new experience in the life of the family.

In appearance William Lane was a brown-toned,

brown-eyed lad, whose colouring formed a strong contrast to that of the blue and hazel-eyed Alcotts. Louisa, the lover of novelty, admired him for it. " A brown boy with a William Penn style of countenance," was the description she afterwards gave of him. In behaviour he was a quiet, peaceable lad who made no trouble. Assimilated to the Alcott brood, he accepted his place without question. William had evidently been disciplined by life. He could go to sleep at the most exciting moments, and there were many new exciting moments for him in America.

Louisa had known boys, but never a refined one like William. The Lanes, though the strictest Puritans, were cultivated people and came to America in the character of educated English gentlefolk. This alone would have caused Louisa to regard them with awe. For her, William Lane had background. Louisa had played with boys, but she had never lived on familiar terms with a refined boy in her own home. William was a wholly new experience in boys.

3

The elder Lane came to America with Bronson Alcott as an adventurer in what he would have termed the life of the spirit. He left his well-established school in Surrey, England, to follow the light of a new prophet in a strange country. Like so many who came into contact with Alcott and felt the influence of his personality, he deemed that nothing else in life was so much worth while as simply to be near his inspiration. He believed he had found in Alcott a brother, a successor to his recently dead friend, and an inspired lifelong leader.

In the year 1843 Charles Lane and Bronson Alcott together founded Fruitlands, or the New Eden. Lane bought the farm in Roxbury in early spring, and the colony took possession on the 1st of June. It started off hopefully and with all the outward signs of success. But Emerson, who visited them in the summer, made this shrewd observation in his journal: " They look well in July; we will see them in December." His direful premonition proved all too true, for when December came, the colony had practically ceased to exist. The New Eden had not produced sustenance for the winter and had begun to break up in October. Whatever or whoever may have been to blame — and mutual reproaches were plentiful — there had been of course little possibility of a margin the first winter. The colony had been too hopeful. When hard times came, the members disappeared one by one until only the Lanes and the Alcotts were left. Came then the bitter-cold months of December and January, during which, walled in by snow-banks and battered by wintry blasts, the founders had to grapple with the desperate problem of what to do next.

The outcome is generally known. First the Lanes departed forever and after them the Alcotts *in toto* withdrew. This was the final and definitive desertion of Fruitlands. The gay phalanstery of the summer had

AMOS BRONSON ALCOTT

from a pastel portrait made about 1852
Courtesy of Little, Brown and Company

absolutely vanished, to be remembered only in history, leaving only a solitary empty farmhouse to tell the tale.

Yet Lane's trip to America did not terminate with the New Eden. Leaving his son with the Shakers at the near-by village of Harvard, he continued his wanderings. He lived for a time at the socialist colony in Red Bank, New Jersey, and later he opened a school in New York. From New York he sailed for England, and his later life disappeared gradually in the hazy English distance.

Notwithstanding the monumental failure of Fruitlands, Lane left some positive landmarks behind him in his American path. For one thing, he succeeded in rescuing the place from " falling back into individuality," as he termed it, for he sold it for a nominal price to people who kept it going as a free community. He also bestowed, involuntarily, a valuable library on his American friends. The many books he had brought with him were never taken back to England, but remained in and around Concord and exercised a permanent mystical influence on the writings of Alcott and Emerson.

4

One of Lane's principal gifts to America was his influence on Louisa May Alcott. He was one of her early teachers, and after her father, her most important one. Bronson Alcott turned the older children's education entirely over to Charles Lane while Lane lived with the family. Though Louisa never expressly acknowledged her debt, she owed a great deal to Lane's extensive culture and attainments. There was of course another aspect of the Englishman which she preferred to forget, and in forgetting this she forgot the educator.

His greatest mark upon her life was made through the Fruitlands colony. Louisa was just ten and a half years old when she moved into this amazing community. But as long as summer lasted, she was happy in spite of things being rather peculiar. It was when the break-up arrived and the Alcotts and the Lanes were left together in the house that her young soul suffered. In October came a forewarning: "We did not have any school, and played in the woods and got red leaves. . . . I wish . . . we were all a happy family this day." By November the depression had deepened. " Father and Mr. Lane had a talk, and father asked us if *we* saw any reason for us to separate. Mother wanted to, she is so tired. I like it, but not the school part or Mr. Lane." In December she wrote: " Mr. Lane was in Boston, and we were glad. In the eve father and mother and Anna and I had a long talk. I was very unhappy and we all cried. Anna and I cried in bed, and I prayed God to keep us all together."

Step by step the children went through the emotional crisis with their elders. Louisa prayed that her father might not leave them and go away with Mr. Lane. For this was the terror which now added itself to the other great fear — the fear of want, cold, and solitude. The children could not understand why this catastrophe threatened, but they knew that their mother considered the danger a real one. Shut off from all the outside world and every balancing and sane influence that might have come in that way, the little group, including the children, lived through a strenuous crisis that inevitably left deep scars. For children with undeveloped and sensitive nerves, it was an especially cruel experience. Louisa had just entered her twelfth year and was in that tentative and transient age when outside storms do the most damage.

It must have been a tense moment when the two Lanes, father and son, departed. Did Lane say anything to Abba in leaving, or did he give any sign of farewell to Bronson? Did he go on foot or by sled? And did William, who went to sleep at crucial moments, have to be waked up to go with his father? The departure is shrouded in silence. One only knows that the English pair went away at last to the Shaker colony, definitely and positively, and did not come back again.

Then Bronson Alcott did an unexpected thing that brought more misfortune. He threw himself on his bed and refused to get up again. He declined to speak or eat or drink for days and days, and the time dragged on despairingly while he lay there in his despondency. The children's terror grew. Were they, after all the incredible stress and strain, and at the moment, too, when relief seemed in sight, to lose their father? For they believed that Bronson was going to die. This anxious time was heaped on top of the sufferings they had just come through, before the throbs and pangs of the last crisis had subsided. They survived it as they survived most things — by virtue of that hidden amalgam which enabled the Alcott family, in spite of every thrust of misfortune, to come through together.

One day Bronson got up from his bed, and the pilgrims moved on. Six months of Fruitlands had done what years otherwise could scarcely have done to the family. People often speak of Fruitlands in connection with Louisa's life as an experience which lasted two or three years.

5

At their next sojourn, a tiny crossroads known as Still River, the children lived for the first time in their lives as other children do. They went to the district school and played with their schoolmates. The teacher of the district school, Miss Chase, was no oracle, but just a school-teacher. The neighbours were not poets and sages, but ordinary people with unimportant affairs into which the children threw themselves with warmhearted interest or into which they blundered to their cost. The neighbours in turn treated them like any other children who might come their way. The Alcotts occupied a house with a family named Lovejoy. " I remember . . . Mr. Lovejoy," said May Alcott afterwards; " we were scolded." Mr. Lovejoy, a farmer, treated the little prodigies as if they were common children.

There were large families thereabouts, and the youthful element of the neighbourhood used to congregate indiscriminately in the various barns and wood-sheds. It was a great contrast to the over-mature life the Alcott children had lived at Fruitlands. They spent one whole summer thus with scarcely any supervision of their manners and morals. Even their sacred diaries were neglected.

The four girls were becoming individualities. Anna, or Annie, as her playmates called her, was gentle, domestic, and imaginative. Louisa, or Lu, was more than ever a tomboy, and talented. Elizabeth, " Lizzie," was a quiet child, but friendly. Abba May, " Abbie " then and afterwards " May," was the youngest, spoilt on that account and on account of her beautiful hair. Abbie already began to show that tendency toward correctness which the last of a line of unconventional people might show. Each of the girls " went with," as they phrased it, some other little girl of the same age in the neighbourhood. Even Louisa, who usually played alone, had a " best friend " that summer. They all gave themselves over to the life of Still River without reservations.

She still played with boys, but differently. When the children held a wedding in the wood-shed, Louisa was the bride, and the brother of her " best friend " was the groom. She wore a white apron for a veil, and one of the boys performed the marriage ceremony, pronouncing the couple man and wife. The groom was probably the stout amiable youth who, in Louisa May Alcott's reminiscences, used to stand in the middle of the strawberry patch and let himself be fed with strawberries. His sweet disposition — if this was he — did not preserve the mock union, however. For, according to Louisa's reminiscences, " we slapped one another soon afterwards, finding that our tempers did not agree."

Louisa was wilder than ever for the next year or two. The removal of the dragon of Fruitlands sent her mercurial temperament bounding to a great height. She was entering a period of life which intensified her usual moods. She developed into a tease and a scold; she teased her youngest sister mercilessly and scolded her oldest sister vigorously. Little Abbie's childish mispronounciations came in for a deal of rallying and Annie's adolescent dreaminess was fiercely ascribed to laziness. Only quiet Elizabeth was spared. Louisa joined with the other children in strange forbidden pranks. " I have not forgotten the ten matches we lit on a certain night, and my head and bones still ache after the beating we got," she wrote back to her " best friend " after she had left Still River. Her language was not transcendental. " I need not tell you we are all alive and kicking, most of our family, that is," she wrote to this friend.

It is not surprising that when Abba Alcott got the Still River children together for a play, she assigned the part of the wild Indian girl to Louisa. In an appropriate costume and with her face and arms stained with berry juice, Louisa sang dramatically the popular song: " Wild roved an Indian girl, sweet Alfarata," and drank deeply of the applause and success of that evening.

That Still River summer brought, oddly enough, another quiet boy into the Alcott household to take the place left vacant by William Lane. He came down from Boston as a summer boarder. This was another motherless boy, and he spent not only that summer but many summers afterwards with the Alcotts. He bore the resounding name of Frederick Llewellyn Hovey Willis, but to the Alcott children he was Fred Willis. Abba Alcott made a great pet of him, and Louisa rather shyly followed her lead.

6

Another winter came and went at Still River. The elder Alcotts continued in the same state of suspended animation in which they had left Fruitlands. Abba spent a great deal of time in Boston, and Bronson was cutting wood for Mr. Lovejoy. The children continued to enjoy the ways of ordinary children.

But this was not the kind of simplicity that Bronson and Abba Alcott desired for their offspring. As little did they desire it for themselves. Plain living without high thinking was not to their taste. Quietly they were grooming themselves for another flight into idealism;

and early in 1845, a year and a half after they had left Concord, they went back again. The New Eden and its dramatic downfall were things of the past.

Their return was accompanied by a thrilling adventure. When they left Concord, they had ambled out of the village in a large farm wagon drawn by one horse. In the meantime trips between Still River and Boston had been made by Abba in a stage with outside and inside passengers. But the return trip to Concord was accomplished by the most phenomenal method of transport of all. The Alcotts arrived by way of the new Boston and Fitchburg railroad. The act was characteristic of the family. On their first adjournment to Concord they had patronized the best hotel in town. Now they made their second début in the village and arrived in the grand new steam-cars. It was a true Alcottian flourish.

What had made the removal possible was some money which Abba had inherited from her father, the old Colonel, who had recently died. With this Abba had bought a house near the Emersons, and since she did not have quite enough money for the purchase, Emerson gave her the rest. The Alcotts were going to possess a dignified and stable domicile at last, and just for their own family.

7

Then followed the amazing return of Charles Lane. The tall, sharp-nosed, hard-featured man came striding up the garden path one day and knocked confidently at the Alcotts' door. He had come on the invitation of Mrs. Alcott. After their bitter quarrel at Fruitlands, after all the harsh words and scathing reproaches which had then passed between them, and after the terrible ordeal of their parting, Abba had asked Lane to return as casually as if nothing had happened, and Lane had accepted her invitation in a similar spirit. To Alcott's great credit it may be said that he went away at once on business and allowed his friend and his wife to conduct the place without him. We know from Louisa's letters that her father was in New York most of that summer and that Mr. Lane was her teacher. He took up his residence in Alcott's house and resumed his old duties as if they had never been interrupted, becoming teacher, music-master, and moral guide to the children.

Autumn came; the grapes were ripe; the woods had turned a glorious red and yellow. Still that strange Mr. Lane showed no signs of departing. "We are dreadful wild people here in Concord," wrote Louisa to her best friend in Still River; "we do all the sinful things you can think of, — such as climbing apple-trees and tearing one's clothes off, playing break-neck tag, and shouting and singing in the woods." These things, needless to say, happened outside and beyond the purview of Abba and Mr. Lane. The garden ran down — a lamentable development for a vegetarian family; but, as Louisa said, "Mr. Lane does not understand gardening very well." Then gradually there grew up a state of discord in the fine new house. It seemed that Abba and Mr. Lane were again disagreeing about things. In the late fall, Mr. Lane at last moved away, grumbling rather impolitely at his hostess for her unwillingness to live on a higher plane, sinking the individual in the mass. Then Bronson Alcott came home.

For Louisa, who wished to see everything through her mother's eyes, this reinstatement of the dragon was devastating. Her letters and diaries of that summer show how piteously distracted was her state of mind. If her mother, having once demolished the beast, had turned the sword in his body, all would have been plain sailing. But she saw now that the relation between the three grown-ups was a more complicated situation than she had had any idea of and it gave her the feeling of a nerve-racking dilemma. She wrestled precociously with her mother's contradictory character, and the struggle made her sometimes despondent and sometimes reckless. The departure of Mr. Lane brought her providential relief.

CHAPTER IV

The Happiest Years

THE CONCORD houses along the Lexington Road were all of the same type as the Old Manse, though of less imposing dimensions. Those along the Lexington Road were single-chimney houses. Someone had thought of building there against the sheltered hillside, and others had followed the pioneer's example. A string of houses followed, snugly backed against the hill and looking out over the lush meadows to southward. From the front windows of these houses one caught the last glimpse of the stage departing for Boston.

A graphic impression of this part of Concord is conveyed by the opening description in *Jo's Boys,* where "a pretty brown cottage" is pictured as "nestling among the trees." A little to the westward a "white-pillared mansion " was the Emerson house. The brown cottage was the home of the Alcotts.

Life in Concord in the middle of the nineteenth century was a combination of rusticity and intellectuality — plain living and high thinking. Farm people and refugees from the city formed the population. A simple social life pervaded the town. The river was a popular resort, and everyone who could afford it kept a private boat. Boating parties in the summer and skating parties in the winter formed the principal social pleasures of the village. Evening parties, at which games with forfeits were played and the lancers danced, furnished a meeting-place for the simple and the great. The atmosphere of the place was distinctly creative; nor was this tone supplied entirely by the writers and artists who had settled there. The inventor of the Concord grape was one of the truly representative spirits of the town and had his rightful place in the inspired community. Occasionally there are such little democracies of genius in the world, and Concord in the middle of the nineteenth century was an outstanding example of the kind.

Probably this only happens in a town with a past. Concord was steeped in history. It had its Revolutionary battle, its Old Manse, and its ancient names and fames. Descendants of the people who had created great traditions still lived on the spot. Concord was settled, seasoned, aged. It had an accumulated back-

THOREAU'S HUT, WHICH ALCOTT HELPED BUILD

from a drawing by May Alcott

ground of more than two hundred years. Its American soil was rich.

The house which the Alcotts moved into in 1845 was one of the row of brown houses on the Lexington Road. They named it appropriately " Hillside." A large central chimney, a square front hall, and four large rooms — two above and two below — formed the main part of the dwelling. A wide kitchen fireplace on the rear side of the chimney opened into a long narrow lean-to chamber. " Before Mr. Alcott took it in hand," says Hawthorne, who owned it afterwards, " from the style of its construction, it seems to have survived beyond its first century. He added a porch in front, and a central peak, and a piazza at each end, and painted it a rusty, olive hue, and invested the whole with a modest picturesqueness." Alcott did even more than this; he cut the barn in two and added it to each side of the house, he dug terraces out of the great hill, planted fruit trees, and laid out his usual fine garden. When he had completed his improvements, the place, says Hawthorne, was an attractive residence which people always noticed in passing.

In this brown house Louisa May Alcott lived from her thirteenth to her sixteenth year. She afterwards said that she spent here " the happiest years of her life." The house itself, as it was then, before Hawthorne or even Alcott had made any changes, was immortalized as the background of *Little Women,* where it lives forever in the form in which the sixteen-year-old Louisa May Alcott knew it.

2

Louisa would never have called her " happiest years " years that were not the happiest for the whole family. But Hillside seems to have meant good times for all of them. Alcott was happy in his reunion with Emerson; Abba was vastly proud of " her house "; and the four young girls were just at the age when most harmony prevailed among them. The eldest was not too old nor the youngest too young to join together in a common play-group. The spirit of Hillside was the spirit of *Little Women*, though the ages of the sisters were moved upward in the story. Louisa recalled that spirit in after years as the golden age of the Alcotts.

Louisa and Anna, thirteen and fourteen, went to the district school. It was a very susceptible age to be launched in a public school, but Bronson Alcott, true to his preference for teaching younger children, had lost interest in their education about this time. There were social consequences of importance to his daughters. They met other girls of their own age. These were at first a little shy of them on account of their father's reputation and their own reputation as prodigies, but they gradually made friends. At least the girls made friends with Anna. They also saw for the first time a real live young man school-teacher. They had previously met in the schoolroom only their somewhat elderly father and the equally elderly Charles Lane.

The young schoolmaster, John Hosmer, was, moreover, tarred with the same brush which had stroked Alcott and Lane; he had been a resident at Brook Farm if not at Fruitlands. John Hosmer and the odd Alcott girls had this unconventional background in common. It helped to make a social contact between them. This again was more useful to gentle Anna than it was to fierce Louisa.

There was still no softening or blossoming in Louisa; she remained a hoyden. She could vault a fence like a boy and did it frequently in spite of her longer skirts. Her mother called her "wild," and Louisa obediently then called herself "wild." She might do something to atone for being wild, but not to be wild would be to fly in the face of the omniscient. She took one of her younger schoolmates sleigh-riding by the simple expedient of untying a strange horse from its hitching-post, climbing into the sleigh, and driving off. The terrified little girl, hypnotized by such daring, climbed into the sleigh with her and lived to tell the tale long afterwards. Another thing that "wild Louisa" did was to dress like a boy on all possible occasions. These were usually limited to plays and charades in the barn and at parties; but, tired of these limitations, she was once known to disguise herself as a male and stand in the road outside her gate, talking to one of her sisters. People who passed by in the twilight were properly fooled, as she intended them to be. Her little extravagances were passed over by the townspeople, however, for it was obvious to all that Louisa was good-natured. To see her trundling her two small sisters in a wheelbarrow around the garden was enough to show how genuinely innocent and spontaneous her high spirits were.

The family was her world. Pa and Ma, Annie, Lizzie, and Abbie were her universe. She was jealously possessive of them, collectively and individually. It annoyed her when her sister Annie seemed to fall in with the ways of the Concord group and become one of the crowd. Once when they were at a party, a boy kissed Annie in a game of forfeits. Louisa flew into a rage at his impertinence. She continued long afterwards to abuse him whenever his name was mentioned, never once seeming in the least to suspect any co-operation on the part of Annie. Boldness of this kind was entirely out of the range of her imagination; she could only conceive of Annie's part as timidity. The boy who had kissed Annie was a raider. Louisa, rising in her strength, came to the defence of her sister, straining her young thews and sinews for the task that was always to absorb most of her life — the defence of one Alcott or another against the onslaughts of the world.

Ten-year-old Lizzie was a real little girl who had not yet been canonized by her all-too-human sister. Lizzie, more than Annie or Louisa, made friends with the neighbours. She was a socialized child, as one sees by her journal. " Ellen and Edith Emerson came to see us. I went home with them. When I got back I walked with Abbie by Mr. Bull's to Mrs. Richardson's and drew her baby in the little wagon." A gentle spirit was Lizzie, but withal a flesh-and-blood presence who ran in and out of the houses of the neighbours.

Abbie, the youngest child, still called by her mother " the baby," had all her lessons from her father. Abbie, the future artist, left a little vignette of the family on the Fourth of July 1848, in a letter she wrote her mother. " O Mother, it is so beautiful this morning as I sit in the schoolroom by Father; such bright sunshine all about. . . . I spelt 30 words all right. . . . Father read me some pretty stories about roses, how the little boy was impatient to see the colors, and so picked the bud open, and the leaves withered. . . . Father has your miniature on his desk where he can see it as he opens his desk every morning. As you look stately . . . I wish you would come home soon. . . . We went to the fire-works last evening. They were before Col. Shat-tuck's house on the Common, and all the Concord people (to say ' folks ' seems countrified) were there; some came in chaises and sat in them to see the fire-works go up. Father took us all to see them and we stood before the Court House by the wall to look. . . ." Abbie, at eight, already hated not being in a chaise like the others. " The boys cracked off powder crackers all about us. One almost hit my heel." The spoilt note of mother's " baby " in Abbie comes out.

Aside from Louisa's testimony, we know that life at Hillside was tolerable for the Alcotts. They had a well-built and comfortable house and it was sufficiently and gracefully furnished. Alcott's garden and orchard were productive. The family were regularly treated to little donation parties, as ministers' families are in some communities. Such gifts were habitual. Emerson dropped in at crucial times and left a twenty-dollar bill under a book or a candlestick when he went away. A cheerful Dr. Winship from Roxbury, a relative of Mrs. Alcott's, frequently arrived with clothes — clothes that had to be made over, it is true, but perfectly good for that purpose. Dr. Winship was a great favourite with the Alcott sisters, for he came, said Anna, " like Santa Claus," not like one who comes to the door shouting: " Now I will do good to the poor." Besides being the sisters' master of the wardrobe, he was Louisa's literary adviser. He carried pocketfuls of her manuscripts away with him, showed them about, and spread the rumour of her talent, thus building up her first literary reputation.

The one who derived the least from this Concord life was Abba Alcott. Her old friends were in Boston and she made no friends in the town. Whenever she wanted congenial society, she took the stage for Boston and immersed herself completely in old city associations. Coming back to her family after such interludes, she found the same difficult present always confronting her: a husband without employment and no prospect of getting any; four growing girls with their expanding needs; and a position of dependency and social isolation for herself in the village. With her intense nature,

Abba could not long endure great pressure without trying to do something about it. After three years of Concord she decided to defy fate. The others, including
even her ally, Louisa, might have gone on indefinitely
floating with the tide — and incidentally surviving —
if Abba had not willed that life had to be different.

She was in this frame of mind when a friend from the
city one day dropped in to see her. Lonely and bur-
dened by troubles as she was, she felt too strongly the
relief of seeing all at once a friendly countenance. The
tears began to flow. " Abby Alcott, what does this
mean? " asked her visitor. Abba poured out the tale of
her woes. " Come to Boston and I will find you employment," said her friend, who happened to be an up-to-
date, decisive woman. Abba agreed to do this, and so
the step was taken that initiated a new cycle in the life
of the family.

3

While living at Hillside, Louisa rounded off the last
of her education. When she went away she was ready
to become a wage-earner. In fact, she had already begun earning before the hegira.

The best training of this period she owed to Charles
Lane. Though his work on her mathematics and music
was wasted, he left a permanent imprint on her English
style. He taught her to write Platonic dialogue with
ease. Lane set her composition themes like the following: " A conversation between Themistocles, Aristides,

and Pericles on the proposed appropriation of the funds of the Confederacy of Delos for the ornamentation of Athens." What Louisa could not do with cube root or the piano, she could do with her pen. As long as it was a matter of writing, tasks like the above, which might have struck terror to the soul of a better student, only spurred Louisa on to her best effort. She did them, as she modestly admitted in after life, very well. Substitute for a conversation between the Greeks a conversation between Meg, Jo, Beth, and Amy on the proposed celebration of Christmas without funds, and the far-reaching influence of Mr. Lane as a teacher echoes down the ages. Conversations — written, not spoken — became a part of Louisa's equipment for life. If Charles Lane had trained her to write description during that impressionable summer, what might ultimately have happened to Louisa's fame gives ground for speculation.

But whoever it was that tried to teach her foreign languages made a worse job of it. " I nearly died of German," she said of that tongue. She left a complete proof of her suffering in the name of one of her most famous characters, Professor Bhaer — a name which, derived from no language, has established itself nevertheless as German. Happily received by thousands, nay, millions of readers, Professor Bhaer's name, one feels, could not possibly have been spelled in any other way.

Louisa was never a student; she was too undisciplined to be a student. As an artist she need not have regretted it, but she did regret it and was always a little envious of those she called "learned ladies." But she was almost an insensate reader, chiefly of novels. She read Dickens with the greatest enthralment, each story as it came out. The whole family read Dickens; he came to fill the place with the family once occupied by *Pilgrim's Progress*. As the girls had dramatized and acted the latter, they took on the novels of Dickens to dramatize and act in the same way. Louisa and her sisters turned themselves into Dickens characters and actually adopted their names. Louisa learned to write Dickensese so naturally she could not stop writing it when she wanted to.

Night and day Louisa dreamed her dreams. Most of them were about fame. On seeing a portrait of Jenny Lind in the paper, she wrote in her journal: " She must be a happy girl. I should like to be as famous as she is." Then she added, as a wondering afterthought: " Anna is very happy," for Anna was not famous. As for herself, Louisa hoped that she would one day be as famous as Jenny Lind, and when that day came she had no doubt that she, too, would be happy. It was one of the day-dreams in which, without let or hindrance from anyone, she ceaselessly indulged herself.

4

At fifteen Louisa wrote. She was at fifteen an author. Allowing for the fact that most of what she wrote consisted of trite poems and sentimental fiction which almost any bright girl of her age might have turned out, her attitude toward writing was that of a worker. She wrote her poems and stories regularly and it never occurred to her not to write them. The end of this preoccupation of hers was that she sometimes turned out something good.

She achieved then the easy touch, the professional accent, the surety and flow that ultimately mark the conscious author. A comparison of one of Louisa's poems with one of her mother's shows the difference between her work and the work of an amateur. Mrs. Alcott gave Louisa a pen on her fourteenth birthday and composed a poem to go with it. Poems were usually composed in the Alcott family for birthdays and anniversaries. Mrs. Alcott's poem for this occasion ran:

> Oh, may this pen your muse inspire,
>   When wrapt in pure poetic fire,
> To write some sweet, some thrilling verse;
>   A song of love or sorrow's lay,
> Or duty's clear but tedious way
>   In brighter hope rehearse.
> Oh, let your strain be soft and high,
>   Of crosses here, of crowns beyond the sky;
> Truth guide your pen, inspire your theme
>   And from each note joy's music stream.

Soon afterwards Louisa wrote the verses that she eventually published unchanged in *Under the Lilacs*, entitled " My Kingdom." Her poem ran:

A little kingdom I possess,
    Where thoughts and feelings dwell,
And very hard I find the task
    Of governing it well.
For passion tempts and troubles me,
    A wayward will misleads
And selfishness its shadow casts
    On all my words and deeds.

How can I learn to rule myself,
    To be the child I should —
Honest and brave — nor ever tire
    Of trying to be good?
How can I keep a sunny soul
    To shine along life's way?
How can I tune my little heart
    To sweetly sing all day?

Dear Father, help me with the love
    That casteth out my fear!
Teach me to lean on thee, and feel
    That thou art very near;
That no temptation is unseen,
    No childish grief too small,
Since thou, with patience infinite,
    Doth soothe and comfort all.

I do not ask for any crown,
    But that which all may win;
Nor seek to conquer any world
    Except the one within.
Be thou my guide until I find,
    Led by a tender hand,
Thy happy kingdom in *myself,*
    And dare to take command.

By their lilt and simplicity, the verses show that the family impulse toward literary creativeness was working out in Louisa at last. The distributed talents of the group became sharpened and focused and unified in the devotion of the one.

Louisa's sister Anna was writing fiction almost as busily and almost as well as Louisa in those days. They both modelled their stories on those they read in the popular weekly papers — journals which represented not a high ideal, perhaps, but an actual market for that which they hoped to write. They imitated their models successfully. Anna once read aloud to her family a story of her own composing, while pretending to read it from a Boston paper; and the family never suspected the hoax. Louisa went a step further; a story that she wrote at sixteen, after lying around for a few years, was finally sold to one of the weekly journals. Both girls could write melodramatic fiction with extreme fluency and prolificness.

Their greatest skill was shown in their plays, on which they collaborated. No one knew, scarcely they themselves, where Louisa left off in these plays and Anna began, or the reverse. They wrote, produced, and acted their dramas without the aid of anyone else. As Anna afterwards testified, they " usually acted the whole play, each assuming five or six characters, and with rapid change of dress becoming in one scene a witch, a soldier, a beauteous lady, and a haughty noble." They often introduced " into one short scene, a bandit, two cavaliers, a witch, and a fairy spirit — all enacted by two people." Sometimes the exigencies of production required them both to take the same part in different scenes of the play. But usually the author-actor-producers were able to avoid this awkwardness. " Long speeches were introduced to allow a ruffian to become a priest." They planned and executed elaborate stage effects, with thunder, lightning, towers, costumes, and music. No requirement of plot, character, or scenery seemed to daunt them. Tragedy and comedy were equally undertaken. Louisa played well and Anna, Louisa said, played better, but there was no jealousy between them. Their performance was one of great promise, and the training imparted was of a highly disciplinary character.

Some of their best plays and productions belong to the Hillside period. The play described in *Little Women* appears to be a combination of *The Captive of Castile* and *The Witch's Curse,* two of their favourites which were written at that time. The episode of the cot-bed's collapsing dates them, for it was at Hillside, according to Fred Willis (the summer boarder), that the cot-bed collapsed and the tower fell. The rest of the whole magnificent series — *The Greek Slave; Bianca; The Unloved Wife; or, Woman's Faith; The Bandit's Bride* — must also have been written then, when Anna and Louisa were respectively a little over and a little under sixteen. Commenting on their state of mind from the superior ground of maturity, one of them, Anna, afterwards said: " The children accomplished a play full of revenge, jealousy, murder, sorcery, of all of which indeed they knew nothing but the name. . . . These ' Comic Tragedies ' . . . are most characteristic of the young girls whose lives were singularly free from the experiences of many maidens of their age. Of the world they knew nothing; lovers were ideal beings, clothed with all the beauty of their innocent imaginations. Love was a blissful dream; constancy, truth, courage, and virtue quite everyday affairs of life. . . ."

It was in this life of her imagination, romantic and absurd as it was, that Louisa found her reality. Anna might let her fancy stray from phantom lovers to mundane boys once in a while, even to the point of allowing a rough lad to kiss her; but Louisa's fancy clung fast to the noble images of her own creating, and her emotions were directed toward her own fantasies and dreams. She was most herself when she was giving them form and direction by writing or acting.

5

Certain overwrought fantasies fastened upon Louisa in the summer of 1848 which make one think it was best for her to be dragged off to Boston in the fall and put to work. The emotional girl was in a ferment of dreams without practical outlet or objective relief in her life.

Her life-purpose, as she envisaged it — " to give her mother the comfort and ease which she had never known in her married life " — eliminated marriage. Unconsciously she had been moving in that direction for a long time. At the age of ten she had written in her journal: " Father asked us what was God's noblest work. Anna said *men,* but I said *babies.* Men are often bad; babies never are." Now her unconscious motive was becoming conscious; she felt that men were dangers to be avoided and that marriage was a trap in which noble women like her mother were caught and held. She was ready to become a knight-errant and rescue the fallen princess at all costs. And not at all costs either, for she wanted fame to accompany her great sacrifice; but for her supreme purpose in life she was ready to pay and to suffer all else.

Denying herself love, Louisa had to turn to worship. This she did rather easily by adoring her father's nearest friend, Emerson. " I wrote letters to him," she says, " but never sent them; sat in a tall cherry-tree at midnight, singing to the moon till the owls scared me to bed; left wild-flowers on the door-step of my ' Master.' " Her behaviour, modelled on some obscure idea of herself as Mignon, did not last long, for it did not satisfy her. Louisa had a very hearty desire for an audience; she did not enjoy composing tributes which no one ever saw or making presents which no one ever acknowledged. She soon transferred her devotion to Emerson's daughter, Ellen, to whom she gave, not anonymous gifts of wild-flowers, but tributes of a less private nature in a series of *Flower Fables* she wrote for her. The fables were circulated, admired, and finally published. Their sentimental tenuousness was a great contrast to the vigorous romanticism of the *Comic Tragedies*. But the *Flower Fables* were better suited to the taste of her sentimental time. Her soul-suffering about Emerson ended in a little published book that gave her the beginning of a literary reputation.

CHAPTER V

Boston

IN the early history of the United States, Boston was twenty-five or thirty years ahead of the rest of the country in development. It had more culture than the average American city in the middle of the nineteenth century. To this day it presents an atmosphere of literacy wholly unique, as, for instance, even the roadside signs for motorists bear witness, implying, as they do, that only well-educated people drive automobiles in and around Boston. Later developments have not destroyed the flavour of the early Massachusetts Bay colony. The refinement of the Pilgrims had a primitive hold that always persists.

This was impressively visible in the decade before the Civil War. Prosperous, complex, sophisticated, Boston led an isolated life on the upper Atlantic seaboard. It had the involved social conditions of one of the older European cities. It was more like Manchester than New York. A large community, it had well-defined problems of organization when other American cities were still in the inchoate state of pioneer crowds.

Among other organized functions which Boston had developed before the Civil War was organized philanthropy. The visiting lady bountifuls with their baskets and warm flannels had given place to paid charity visitors. The innovation met a twofold demand: it organized relief and furnished a much-needed new occupation for women. It was one of these newly created positions that Abba Alcott's friend secured for her.

A perverse vision had come to Mrs. Alcott while still in Concord. Both of her older daughters were earning wages. Anna was teaching away from home, and Louisa had begun to teach also, having opened a school in the barn. By a reversal of the usual process between parents and children, the girls set an example for their middle-aged mother. Mrs. Alcott, having steadily refused to see the necessity for working prior to her marriage when the necessity for it had been most apparent, now all at once saw it very clearly. Just when her family needed her attention most, she decided to go forth and become a wage-earner. Their finances had not become any worse, because Anna and Louisa had begun to bring a little money into the home. But Mrs. Alcott's heroism drove her just at that point to take her spectacular plunge into a life of wage-earning.

The Alcott family moved to Boston and Abba Alcott was a paid charity visitor for several months. One can imagine that, for a woman who had never worked before, the job was something of an ordeal. She climbed tenement stairs and wrote reports on her work — so modern had charity become in Boston in those days. Her reports are said to have been excellent and to have embodied some valuable suggestions, but the documents themselves appear to have vanished and only their reputation has survived. Mrs Alcott's best-known contribution to the subject of charity is the revised proverb often quoted as Mrs. Alcott's by her daughter Louisa: " Cast your bread upon the waters and it will return to you buttered." Her cynicism, though it need not be taken too seriously, was native and it did not help her to climb tenement stairs or suffer gladly the hardships of a charity visitor's life.

Mrs. Alcott then opened an intelligence office. Her work among the poor had brought her in contact with the immigrants of Boston and the kind of homes which produced the city's domestic servants. Her idea was that she could make use of her natural position as an intermediary between these workers and the ladies of her acquaintance. The plan worked — the plan did not work. Louisa says her mother's intelligence office was a success, but Louisa is not always a trustworthy reporter on her mother's enterprises. The only domestic-service job that Mrs. Alcott secured, as far as we know, is the one she turned over to her daughter Louisa, of which we shall hear more later. She soon gave up the intelligence office and fell back on the time-honoured resource of financially distressed gentlewomen; she took boarders. Besides Fred Willis, who was studying at Harvard, she boarded her nephew and some other students. With this slight addition to her income, she moved the family from the somewhat dingy district of High Street, where they had been living, to a better neighbourhood on Beacon Hill.

During this time of novelty and experiment a great disaster befell them. " We had small-pox in the family," says Louisa, " caught from some poor immigrants whom mother took into our garden and fed one day. We girls had it lightly, but father and mother were very ill, and we had a curious time of exile, danger, and trouble. . . . No doctors, and all got well."

The loneliness of the Alcott family is apparent. Not even a doctor visited them. Time after time the Alcotts seemed to arrive at these painful crises when all the world fell away and left them alone in trouble and in danger. Family bonds of great strength were forged and re-forged at such times.

2

Life was developing for Louisa very unevenly. Though she had dedicated herself to a grown-up responsibility, she was annoyed by the necessity of growing up. She hated the paraphernalia of adult femininity. Gloves, bonnets, and done-up hair gave her terribly to worry. It was easier for her to shoulder a heroic responsibility than to accept a daily routine of hairpins. Precocious in many ways, she was still childishly below her age in many others.

Louisa spent two lost years in Boston while her mother went out to work. For the first time in her life she failed to write in her diary. With Abba too busy to read them, she had no one to whom to address her thoughts. Her journal had always been a sort of correspondence with her mother, who read the pages after she had gone to bed at night and left little notes in reply. Without this response Louisa's confessions ceased to flow. It was not until her mother left off being an outside worker and returned to domestic life again that Louisa's diary was resumed. Testimony more eloquent than this in regard to the trial those two years had been for her could hardly be given.

She began the new record thus: " Boston, May, 1850. — So long a time has passed since I kept a journal that I hardly know how to begin. Since coming to the city I don't seem to have thought much, for the bustle and dirt and change send all lovely images and restful feelings away. Among my hills and woods I had fine free times alone, and though my thoughts were silly, I daresay, they helped to keep me happy and good. I see now what Nature did for me, and my ' romantic tastes,' as people called that love of solitude and out-door life, taught me much."

Nature's education had ceased and the city's education had begun. Social influences in Boston took the place of Concord woods and hills. Women were stepping out quite spectacularly in the old city. It was women who had made it possible to complete the Bunker Hill monument by raising the money needed — a feat which had taken place in 1843, but about which people were still talking in 1850. The great fair by means of which the money had been raised had been an epoch-making influence, making the public realize how important women were. Woman suffrage was actively discussed and petitions were drawn up. Careers for women were much agitated and reforms were put through, resulting among other things in Louisa's mother's employment. Women editors were rising to prominence and women writers were growing famous; nursing was coming to be regarded as a profession; women lecturers and women doctors were prominent, though still outside the pale. A striving girl of seventeen or eighteen, such as Louisa was, felt these social influences all around her and was prepared by her idealistic upbringing to accept them; passively, at least. Shyness always kept her from joining in the active fight.

Louisa had, besides feminist ideals, the courageous example of her sister Anna. After teaching in Concord and Boston, Anna had decided to leave New England and had ventured all the way to Syracuse, New York, to take a teaching position. Though homesick and ill, she stuck to her job and was a pillar of strength to the fam-

ANNA BRONSON ALCOTT
(MRS. JOHN PRATT)

Courtesy of Little, Brown and Company

ily during this period. Anna had made a success of her teaching. They liked her in Syracuse and wanted her to stay there; and Anna, quietly laying aside the cultivation of her talents, stayed. Undoubtedly the sacrifice in Anna's case was real, but she made it easily. Everyone else took it calmly, too, except Bronson Alcott, who, having watched Anna from the first breath that she drew, could not bear the thought of her delicate talents going to waste. But Anna was earning money to help her family. She was not dedicated in her deepest heart to a career, as was Louisa.

And Louisa taught also. She did not like to teach but, because she was conscientious, she probably did it well. " I like it better than I thought," she said, " though it's very hard to be patient with the children sometimes." She, too, had to lay aside poems and stories. " I get very little time to write or think; for my working days have begun. . . ." Firmly she held herself down to this thought. Teaching became more and more for her a serious interest and occupied all of her time. Once again she neglected her daily journal for several weeks and months. Serious, resolute, devoted, she was determined to help the beloved family to which she belonged and which belonged to her. As long as the family was a unit, Louisa felt she could stand anything. She sketched the group one day in colours that were sober but not dreary. " Began school again with ten children. Anna went to Syracuse to teach; Father to the

West to try his luck. . . . Mother had several boarders, and May got on well at school. Betty was still the home-bird," who " had a little romance with C."

While the family lived in the small house in High Street, where Mrs. Alcott first had her intelligence office and later kept boarders, Louisa had a good view of the contrasts of city life. It was near the wharves, and many derelicts were seen thereabouts. Not far away were the fine shops and the grand shop-windows. Louisa, passing these diverse sights on her way to and from her school, took note of each. Toward misery and poverty she had the family attitude, which was that people without money were more or less akin to them. The Alcotts still opened their door, as they had done in Concord, to anyone who knocked. " Our poor little home," said Louisa, " had much love and happiness in it, and was a shelter for lost girls, abused wives, friendless children, and weak or wicked men. Father and Mother had no money to give, but gave them time, sympathy, help; and if blessings would make them rich, they would be millionaires. This is practical Christianity." Passing down High Street and looking into the shop-windows, she never once thought, even transiently, that she had any right to the grand things she saw there. " In the street I try not to covet fine things," she said. All that the city contrasts taught Louisa was that if her family were ever to be rescued from privation and poverty, she would have to rescue them. She dreamed constantly of doing it. " Seeing so much money flying about, I long to honestly get a little and make my dear family more comfortable. I feel weak-minded when I think of all they need and the little I can do." She, Louisa, knight-errant and heroic rescuer of the Alcotts, would alone lead them across the boundary-line which kept them back from plenty and comfort.

Four years after Louisa moved to Boston she sold her first story. " It was written in Concord when I was sixteen," she said. " Great rubbish! " The episode, however, shows her in a role which marks her out definitely as an author and sets her off from her sister Anna, who had written stories that were just as good. Louisa not only had written but had sold a story; and stories were written to be sold. She saw this with her professional eye before she was out of her teens. The practical side of writing had dawned on her. Louisa had a trace of Puritan shrewdness in her otherwise dreamy and idealistic character.

3

It was a sheaf of adventurous years for Louisa's family — this decade before the Civil War. What with Abba's entering the labour market as a wage-earner, Anna's emigrating to Syracuse, and Louisa's having a story published, it behooved Bronson also to show his mettle in some way. And, tradition to the contrary notwithstanding, he did so.

But Bronson's adventure was not really brand-new. It was for him the revival of an old and well-worn practice. To others it may have seemed a daring innovation, but to him months of travel in a strange country were no very great hardship nor very unfamiliar. The experience was one he had already had and enjoyed. Peddling through the South in his youth had made him more or less into a vagabond and he was now able to return to this life in a respectable guise. Following in the traces of Emerson, who set him a brisk example, he went up and down, hither and thither, throughout the expanding West. His pack filled with lectures, or " conversations," as he always called them, he peddled from community to community, enjoying the life thoroughly.

The lecture bureau announced his visit thus: " *Conversations. —* A. Bronson Alcott proposes to discourse, in some of the Western cities, during the current season and coming winter, on THE LEADING REPRESENTATIVE MINDS OF NEW ENGLAND; with suitable Retrospects and Prospects of its History and Tendencies. The course to consist of six evening conversations, to be held at such times and places as shall be designated by card or otherwise hereafter." The representative New England minds which he offered to interpret to the West were Daniel Webster, Horace Greeley, William Lloyd Garrison, Margaret Fuller, Theodore Parker, and Horatio Greenough. He attempted to discuss them as psychological types. Alcott had tried to be scientific about his own children and he also tried to be scientific about his friends and contemporaries. His lectures, had they survived, might be interesting character sketches.

If the well-known portrait of Mrs. Richard Hildreth may be trusted, Alcott was furnished beyond the ordinary with good looks at this time. His manners were courtly and ingratiating and he carried himself with a habitual air of distinction. His partly grey hair was worn a little long, and his clothes had a style of their own with a suggestion of elegance in spite of frayed edges. His manners, his dress, his friendliness toward strangers equipped him well for the career he had entered upon. The subjects of his lectures were attractive; he should have drawn large audiences of New Englanders who were living in homesick exile. In spite of all this his first trip, made in the winter of 1853–4, could not be called a success.

The story of his return has been told dramatically by Louisa. " In February Father came home. Paid his way, but no more. A dramatic scene when he arrived in the night. We were waked by hearing the bell. [The railway station was near by.] Mother flew down, crying ' My husband! ' We rushed after, and five white figures [There were only four; Anna was in Syracuse] embraced the half-frozen wanderer who came in hungry, tired, cold, and disappointed, but smiling bravely and as serene as ever. We fed and warmed and brooded over him, longing to ask if he had made any money; but no one did till little May said, after he had told all the pleasant things, ' Well, did people pay you? ' [May — the spoilt youngest child.] Then, with a queer look, he opened his pocket-book and showed one dollar, saying

83

with a smile that made our eyes fill, ' Only that! — My overcoat was stolen and I had to buy a shawl. [Alcott loved a shawl; he even had his overcoats made with shawls on them.] Many promises were not kept, and travelling is costly; but I have opened the way, and another year shall do better.' I shall never forget how beautifully Mother answered him, though the dear, hopeful soul had built much on his success; but with a beaming face she kissed him, saying, ' I call that doing *very well*. Since you are safely home, dear, we don't ask anything more.' " Did Mrs. Alcott suspect that her husband had found his absence no great personal hardship?

As a matter of fact, Alcott did do better afterwards; but Louisa never told of his subsequent returns. He went again the following winter, and the following, and so on to the end of his life, omitting only the Civil War years. He became a popular lecturer in the West, going as far as Iowa, and made lasting friends wherever he went. He learned to tell the story of his life with amiable humour when people asked him about it. His tours in the West were an important part of his life and a congenial retreat from much that was unavoidably unhappy in it.

4

The adventurous' years, which brought so many changes to the others, brought an unfortunate change to Louisa's sister Lizzie. On Lizzie's young back fell the burden of the housework when Mrs. Alcott went to work. The friendly child who loved the rainbow, the shadows on the brook, the rustling breeze, who wrote the most charming of all the childish diaries, was drafted as the family cook. " Anna and I taught," says Louisa; " Lizzie was our little house-keeper — our angel in a cellar kitchen." Fred Willis, the boy who boarded with the Alcotts for so many years, said: " While the family lived in Boston and Mrs. Alcott was directing her Intelligence offices . . . [Lizzie took] full care of the family kitchen." Lizzie was the family Cinderella.

Still, she was not the altogether selfless angel into which Louisa's tender memory later converted her. She was a natural girl in spite of her shyness. In fact, it is a question whether Louisa was not more shy than Lizzie. A little romance came to the young kitchen-maid, showing that she was not wholly submerged by her pots and pans. The slight flurry was with one of Louisa's pupils, the son of a friend of the family who came from Beacon Street for lessons once a week. So Lizzie, though shut up in the sunless depths of a Boston basement, had her little adventure too.

But because she was at the blossoming age, an age so sensitive, the burden of household duties fell the more heavily upon her. If she came out of the ordeal somewhat reduced in stamina and less able to resist the sickness that later befell her, one need not be surprised at it.

It is difficult to know what Lizzie was like. Her father called her " Psyche," and her sister painted her as the ethereal " Beth "; so we always think of her as spiritual and sylphlike. But Bronson and Louisa both idealized her in their different ways. The only portrait of her that remains is a vague sketch at Orchard House that leaves one in doubt even as to her physical appearance. One can only believe that she had the same talent and gifts as the rest of the family and that her personality, having little opportunity to develop during the Boston years or the year in New Hampshire which followed, faded away with her health.

5

The Boston sojourn of the Alcotts had almost come to an end. They were living in upper Pinckney Street in a house that they had rented. The red-brick house is still standing just as it was when the Alcotts lived in it — with the door opening into a narrow street full of similar red-brick houses. But always for the Alcotts there was the agony of rent. Life was becoming too desperate in the city and it was apparent that the family would have to go back to the country. Alcott wanted to go back to Concord or else to Plymouth, where his friend Marston Watson owned a large estate and offered him inducements to settle. But Abba Alcott, who evidently wished to keep Alcott from his friends, refused to retire either to Concord or to Plymouth and accepted the loan of a house from a kinsman of hers at Walpole, New Hampshire. To Walpole, therefore, the family went in the summer of 1855.

There occurred the grim, heart-breaking tragedy of

all their lives. The two younger girls, Betty, as Lizzie had now come to be called, and Abby, caught the scarlet fever from Mrs. Alcott's visiting some poor children who had it. The children died and Abby and Betty were dangerously ill. In the end Abby recovered completely from the disease, while Betty was left an invalid. Some dread sequela of the sickness overtook her. She failed to improve and remained in delicate health in spite of all that was done for her. After a year it became evident that Betty was wasting away. A sojourn at the seashore was tried, but this, like everything else, only awakened hopes to destroy them. A letter from Mrs. Alcott conveys more eloquently than anything else can the poignancy of the fatal illness and the struggle she was making to arrest its progress. " Elizabeth's condition from day to day has left me in doubt what to write about her," she said. " The first week was warm and pleasant and the change was grateful to her . . . but the last weeks have been cold and rainy and most unfortunate for her. Dr. Newhall thinks it best to remove her directly back, that the comforts of home and the society of the family are now all important to her. Dr. Charles gives a different opinion, that she has in every way failed but that she has not even incipient disease of the lungs. . . . So I shall remain until next month. . . . It seems to me that the system of medicine is a prolonged guess."

They tried as a last resort taking her back to Concord, where as a child she had been happy. Hillside had been sold by Mrs. Alcott to the Hawthornes in 1851; but the money which, by the terms of her father's will, could only be spent for a home for Mrs. Alcott was still intact. With this money the house next door to Hillside, now Wayside, was bought. The place was such a ruin that it was not habitable, so the family moved into temporary quarters near the village green. Here, in the centre of the town, the school-children passed by the house every day; and the invalid relieved her loneliness by making pen-wipers of wool and dropping them out of her window to the children as they passed. As winter progressed, however, she lost strength even for this slight diversion.

Louisa was her sister's faithful night nurse. " Betty loves to have me with her at night, for Mother needs rest," said she. " Strange nights keeping up the fire and watching the dear little shadow try to wile away the long sleepless hours without troubling me," left their woeful impression on the watcher. " In the night she tells me to be Mrs. Gamp, when I give her her lunch, and tries to be gay that I may cheer up." So the two sisters were alone together night after night, sharing the feeling of an inexorable fate that was bearing down, closer and closer, upon them. Louisa, with her excitable disposition, was especially ill-adapted to resist this strain.

At last the sick girl, sensing that the end was near, went through the drear formality of parting. " Tuesday she lay in Father's arms, and called us round her, smiling contentedly as she said, ' All here! ' " The following Sunday, at three o'clock in the morning, she died.

Abba and Louisa were beside her. " A few moments after the last breath came," says Louisa's journal, " as Mother and I sat silently watching the shadow fall on the dear little face, I saw a light mist rise from the body, and float up and vanish in the air. Mother's eyes followed mine, and when I said, ' What did you see? ' she described the same light mist. Dr. Geist said it was the life departing visibly."

Bronson Alcott sat up with the body of his child all night. No one else approached him. His little lost Psyche, who had seemed to him in her infancy the most promising of all his daughters, alone kept him company. One of the brightest auguries of his life had vanished with her loss.

In silence he sustained the blow; but it was not the silence that had fallen upon him at Fruitlands. In the long stretch of intervening years Alcott had learned philosophy. He grieved, but saw no ghosts.

Abba endured desperate pangs of remorse, all the more desperate because she believed that she had brought the fever into the house. It was the great heart-break of her life — as final as the heart-break which Alcott had endured at the break-up of Fruitlands. She never recovered from it.

6

Poor possessive Louisa! Life was doing its bitter best to teach her that facts are facts and have to be borne. While Betty was slipping away from her into eternity, Anna was as surely escaping her by another path.

When the family sadly brought their invalid back to Concord, the Alcott sisters found by a contrariwise fate a pleasanter life awaiting them than they had ever known there. The new school opened by Franklin B. Sanborn was the centre of a lively young society. Despite the shadow overhanging their home, Anna and Louisa entered into this society with enthusiasm. Since its great interest was theatricals, neither Anna nor Louisa could bear to keep out. The Concord Dramatic Union claimed them as soon as they arrived in town. Anna Alcott was its best actress and Louisa was a close second. Youth cannot give itself wholly to sorrow, and while Betty's life was declining to its end, her sisters were earning laurels in the Dramatic Union. " I lead two lives," said Louisa. " One seems gay with plays, etc., the other very sad, — in Betty's room." But there was a still more bitter pill for Louisa in all this gaiety than she at first suspected.

The Concord Dramatic Union was a fairly good stock company, with printed advertisements, programs, and many professional features. One great change from the old Hillside days when Louisa had played the male parts was that, in the new aggregation, there were competent young men to fill these roles. Louisa had to fall back on comedy and character parts, in which she incidentally did very well, developing in time into a popular monologuist. Anna Alcott meantime continued in her old roles as the virtuous wife, the languishing princess, and the threatened virgin. It was her unique social opportunity, for the heroes who now played opposite to her were eligible young men. Anna, though not pretty, was charming and attractive; she was humorous without being satirical; and, no longer exceedingly young, she was gently eager to try what life had in store for her as a woman. In a very short time she had attached one of the young men of the group as a faithful attendant and swain.

Anna Alcott's choice shows what a marriageable young woman she was. It fell upon John Pratt, the son of another Concord family, whose head, before coming to Concord, had been one of the founders of Brook Farm. John Pratt had just returned from the West when he met Anna Alcott, who also had just returned from a similar migration to Syracuse. They were both confirmed New Englanders who had tried the West and come back home to stay. With their similar backgrounds, ideals, and life-adventures, they were from the first a companionable and well-matched pair.

Unlike Anna's first public kiss, which Louisa had so much resented, Anna's relations with John Pratt were masked by the theatrical covering. Louisa's imagination often made it hard for her to distinguish imitation from reality. But the time came to her at last when she saw the facts plainly. " Dear Betty is slipping away," she said in her diary, " and every hour is too precious to waste, so I'll keep my lamentations over Nan's affairs till this duty is over." She duly kept silent, though it was plain throughout the final stages of Betty's illness that Anna and John were lovers. After the funeral Anna Alcott left home to pay a visit to the elder Pratts, who lived on a farm on the outskirts of Concord. Louisa's indignation did not break forth until three weeks after Betty's death. " On the 7th of April, Anna came walking in to tell us she was engaged to John Pratt; so another sister is gone." It was like Louisa's exaggeration to supply the addendum.

Louisa found it hard to forgive her sister. The following autumn she wrote: " My twenty-sixth birthday . . . and a ring of Anna's and John's hair as a peace-offering." As a peace-offering the intertwined gift was singularly ill-chosen. And it did not work. A long engagement followed — an engagement of two years, during which Louisa, though she never doubted John's worth, never became completely reconciled to the marriage. " John is a model son and brother, — a true man, — full of fine possibilities," she wrote, " but so modest one does not see it at once." Somehow one reads between the lines of Louisa's letters and diaries that she did not think the match quite good enough for her sister. Of such false pride Louisa, with all her brightness, was capable. The myth of " the blood of the Mays " was one in which she always took great stock.

After her sister's marriage, her attitude did not change. A visit to the couple during their honeymoon did not help to make matters better. " Saw Nan in her nest," she said, " where she and her mate live like a pair of turtle-doves. Very sweet and pretty, but I'd rather be a free spinster and paddle my own canoe." Louisa was determined not to accept this romance of her sister's or the things that her brother-in-law stood for. He was humorously referred to as the " Prince Consort," or " Darby Coobiddy Esq.," or described by some fantastic appellation; he was seldom spoken of as " John " or " John Pratt " in plain brotherly and sisterly fashion. Her attitudes, once adopted, were hard to change. This one flicked an unfortunate knot in her life-history — one which she never quite untied and which was to cost her eventually much regret and remorse.

Louisa had made up her mind at the age of sixteen that she would be a spinster and have a career. But she had never fully realized what this meant until she saw her *alter ego,* Anna, taking the other course. She had been better prepared for Betty's death; this revelation of life was what she had not been prepared for. In the shock of her discovery, her strong ideal failed her and she wandered for a time miserably in chaos without even dreams for comfort.

CHAPTER VI

Working Girl

LOUISA MAY ALCOTT left home to go to work in the autumn of 1855; but because one of her Boston cousins took her in that winter, she never regarded this as her first actual plunge into the world. The following year she took a furnished room, and this she properly regarded as her first year of independence. The Alcotts had always lived in cousins' houses. In setting up a room of her own, Louisa felt that she had boldly stepped out into the untried. She visited her relations proudly and went home again to her own fireside.

At twenty-five years of age Louisa had fulfilled her promise of becoming an uncommonly tall woman, being only a little under six feet in height. Her hair, dark chestnut in hue, was a yard and a half long. Her eyes were a mixture of blue and hazel, and her complexion was olive. She wore black or claret-colour as a rule, never blue. The style of her dress was plain and quaint, for with her made-over clothes she seldom achieved in those days a smart or fashionable appearance. " Her earnest face, large dark eyes, and expression of profound interest in other things than those which usually occupy the thoughts of young ladies " did not attract young men to her side. In company she had a way of placing herself in a corner and looking out over the heads of the company at what was going on.

Louisa was literally alone in Boston. Hers were among thousands of busy feet that passed through the streets of the city going to or looking for employment. When she went home in the evening, she climbed three or four flights of stairs to a small top-floor room, the windows of which looked out over acres of brown chimney-pots trailing their smoke pennons against the sky. She went out alone in the evenings to lectures, to the theatre, to the charity-class which she taught, in order that she might not lose the habit of good works. She stood where her father had stood thirty years before, with Boston and its effect on her future before her. Bronson himself had not been more earnestly ambitious. Louisa would have said that this was one of the ways in which she was like a boy.

Not the least of her problems was her equivocal social position. " The dear respectable relations," as Louisa once called them, naturally viewed this representative of the clan with suspicion. That a young lady should live in a boarding-house, go out alone, and pay her own way was an unheard-of development in their social circle. Their attitude is best illustrated by an episode noted by Louisa and credited to the sons of her Aunt Bond: "The boys teased me about being an authoress." Louisa had defended herself, saying: "Never mind, I'll be famous yet." Had she inherited less of her mother's pride of blood and ancestry, the situation would have been less of a conflict, and her position less of a problem. As it was, she suffered a good deal from embarrassing moments and found it difficult to maintain her old footing with her relations. They naturally found this singular young woman difficult, and fell into patronizing ways very irksome to Louisa.

The old familiar feeling of privation took on an added pang in the city. Louisa had come to Boston with twenty-five dollars in her pocket. She had earned it by writing stories. Her entire baggage consisted of one small horse-hide trunk. Her old made-over woollens and poplins had done well enough in Walpole and Concord, but in Boston parlours they looked distressingly plain. One of her kindest cousins, Mrs. Lizzie Wells — whose name stands out always pleasantly in Louisa's journal — made her the saving present of a real silk dress. It was the first brand-new silk Louisa had ever had. "I felt as if all the Hancocks and Quincys beheld me as I went to two parties in it on New Year's Eve." A silk dress remained always in Louisa's mind as the prime symbol of elegance, riches, temptation.

She had one profound comfort; she was a natural child of the city. Her solitary tastes were satisfied by being alone in the midst of crowds of strangers. In Concord she had enjoyed wandering alone in the woods; in Boston she went about the streets and tramped around the Common in the same state of musing solitude. In her well-worn clothes and thin shoes she trudged the thoroughfares in the bitterest weather, planning stories and dreaming of the fortune they would one day make for her.

And Louisa was, of course, an intellectual. In her revolt against her father's transcendentalism she strove to escape being an intellectual, but she did not succeed. Her words: " I will make a battering-ram of my head, and make a way through this rough-and-tumble world," show that she was determined to have character, but assumed that she had intellect. The line in her father's sonnet to her which runs:

" Hast with grave studies vexed a sprightly brain "

reveals the little-known fact that Louisa was a serious student. She attended a great many lectures that first winter alone in Boston, for lectures were as common as pies in that city, and someone was always giving her tickets. She liked intellectual pastimes. The theatre was her passion, and by a great stroke of good fortune the manager of the Boston Theatre gave her a pass for the season. She revelled in Lagrange's Norma, Edwin Forrest's Othello, and Edwin Booth's Hamlet. She was taken sometimes by friends to the Boston Museum, a disguised theatre, where Bostonians who thought play-going wicked could see comedies performed in the best manner. Louisa liked to meet the great and the celebrated, and one of her chief pleasures was Theodore Parker's receptions, to which she went steadily, and where she saw many of the species.

But there was nothing of intimacy in all this. In the teeming city she was always solitary.

2

The story of Louisa May Alcott's experiences as a domestic servant has always been told rather apologetically by her historians. She herself tells it without apology in her diary and re-tells it similarly in her fiction. Louisa took two positions of this kind, " living in " and performing the menial duties required of a general houseworker and maidservant.

This happened while Louisa was still in her teens. She was only seventeen when she first went into service. To Mrs. Alcott in her intelligence office a customer came one day asking for a general houseworker. The work he described as light, and the person engaged was to be treated like a member of the family. Louisa happened to be present at the interview and in her impulsive way offered to take the position. The sequel was a sordid bit of exploitation and meanness. She was put to do the most degrading chores, harshly treated, and paid scarcely anything at all. She stuck it out for almost two months, for Louisa did not give up easily. But the experience was one she could never forget, and in one form or another it often bobbed up in her stories.

Her second venture, however, was much happier. She was two years older by this time and more work-seasoned. " In May, when my school closed, I went to Lancaster as second girl. I needed the change, could do the wash, and was glad to earn my $2.00 a week. Home in October with $34.00 for my wages." This was a very spirited and courageous Louisa, who only needed just and reasonable employers to do her work uncomplainingly and give full satisfaction. She apparently did well in this position for an entire season. Then she returned to school-teaching. " After two days' rest, began school again."

In following this kind of life Louisa was merely obeying the custom of New England working girls of an earlier period. A generation or two before her time, girls of good family had worked in the cotton-mills for half the year — in the winter — and had taught school the other half — the summer. Louisa varied the plan a little without changing the spirit. The Puritan ancestry in her came to light in the way she did such things simply and naturally. She followed after her grandfather in being a " last leaf " on the tree of social customs which belonged to an earlier day.

In her experience as a houseworker, however, there was one practical gap. She could not cook. She hated the cook-stove with a hearty and expressive antipathy and detested the kitchen as her natural enemy. Laundry-work, on the other hand, she liked and performed joyously. She wrote a spirited lyric about the wash-tub, entitling it " The Song of the Suds ":

> Queen of my tub, I merrily sing,
>   While the white foam rises high;
> And sturdily wash and rinse and wring,
>   And fasten the clothes to dry;
> Then out in the free fresh air they swing,
>   Under the sunny sky.
>
> I wish we could wash from our hearts and souls
>   The stains of the week away,
> And let water and air by their magic make
>   Ourselves as pure as they;
> Then on the earth there would be indeed
>   A glorious washing-day!

Sewing was another occupation that she followed with ardour. The sewing-machine, just invented, had not yet come into general use. Louisa, like most of the women of her time, spent endless hours stitching interminable seams and hems by hand. And, as she did laundry-work for pay, she also followed sewing as a gainful occupation. Louisa May Alcott was a plain seamstress. " For Mr. Gray . . . a dozen pillow-cases, one dozen sheets, six fine cambric neck-ties, and two dozen handkerchiefs." The price paid her for the whole job was four dollars. " Sewing won't make my fortune," was her rueful comment. She stuck to sewing, however, because she was skilful at it and because she could pursue her dream-life uninterruptedly above the mechanical stitches. " I can do anything with a needle," she said; " I can plan my stories while I work and then scribble 'em down on Sundays." So she patiently carried great piles of sewing up to her sky-parlour and carried them down again when finished, waiting for Sunday to come to grasp her pen with her pricked fingers.

She never tried baby-minding, though her sister Anna was once a nurse. The nearest thing to this that Louisa tried was being a governess. Tutoring came to be her chief dependence, for, as she wrote more and more, she had less time for a class. She had a good deal of trouble finding pupils, for most parents wanted her to teach French, drawing, and music; but she at last found a little lame pupil who occupied her afternoons. This was enough, with her sewing, to support her, and she had the satisfaction of sitting " in a large, fine room part of each day " and looking out on the genteel life of Beacon Street. In the evenings she sewed in her tiny room, by her whale-oil lamp, often far into the night.

All the while she was busy concocting her tales. The first ones were developed out of the plays that she and Anna had written together in the old Hillside days. The stories were written in the same florid and exaggerated style. The weekly papers which had originally trained her in this style of writing now accepted their graduated product at the rate of five and six dollars a story. Her principal customers were the Boston *Saturday Evening Gazette, Gleason's Pictorial Drawing-*

Room Companion, and *Frank Leslie's New York Journal.* But no sooner had Louisa established this market than she began to outgrow it. She soon grew to be somewhat ashamed of her " sensation stories," as she called them, though she continued to write them.

She had presently tasted the elixir of fame. Passing by a news-stand one chill winter's day, she saw a large yellow poster announcing that " *Bertha,* a new tale by the author of *The Rival Prima Donnas* " would appear in the *Saturday Evening Gazette.* She came to a standstill, feeling none of the fierceness of the cold as she read the " delicious words." She read them again and again until her head was giddy with delight and excitement: " The author of *Bertha* and *The Rival Prima Donnas!* " Louisa regretted at the moment none of the long, tedious seams, the thin shoes and shabby clothes, the many backaches and headaches and eye-strains that had brought her to this deliriously happy moment. With difficulty she tore herself away and went on down the street.

But already she was beginning to write with more truth and restraint. The fairy-tales and melodramas which had filled her imagination from childhood had begun to lose some of their charm. She no longer played at story-writing as she and Anna had played when they flung themselves together into the game. The solitary worker has to have a purpose, and Louisa, in her loneliness, had become conscious of one. It was well formulated in her mind when she was twenty-six.

LOUISA MAY ALCOTT

from a daguerreotype made about 1852
Courtesy of Little, Brown and Company

" I hope I shall yet do my great book," she said in her diary; " for that seems to be my work, and I am growing up to it."

Her earnings from all sources, during these first years in Boston, never amounted to more than two hundred dollars a year. The first year she earned only one hundred dollars. Seven years later, after this length of stern and protracted struggle, she was still making less than five hundred dollars a year. At the end of ten years of striving, she was not yet earning as much as a thousand dollars. Not until she was thirty-five years old and had published one book did her income rise to that mark. The great prosperity with which Louisa's name is associated was slow in coming to her.

3

When she returned to Boston in the autumn of 1858, soon after the death of her sister Betty and the engagement of her sister Anna, Louisa found that she could not pick up the dropped threads again. She felt much too tired and discouraged. Work was always hard to find, but now to find it was impossible. Her solitude, which had once been occupied by pleasant dreams, was filled with bitter regrets and failing hopes. Ambition deserted her, and a morbid melancholy took its place. In desolation and despondency she wandered aimlessly in her search for work, and earned nothing.

Immediately after her double loss, Louisa had shown a good deal of wisdom. She had gone up to Boston to look for a new interest. " I had hopes of trying a new life," she said; " the old one being so changed now, I felt as if I must find interest in something absorbing." That was the time when she really came very near to going on the stage. With the courage of desperation, she might have tried it — but " Mr. Barry [the manager of the Boston Theatre] broke his leg," and the accident closed the door she was just opening. Louisa found nothing else that trip that had the same thrill for her and returned dispiritedly to Concord to spend the rest of the summer in brooding and inactivity. " Nature must have a vent somehow," she told herself; but vainly, for still she obtained from her inner self no response in action.

Louisa Alcott relates in her novel called *Work* how she was tempted to commit suicide. The episode — not in the novel, but in actuality — happened while she stood on the old mill-dam in Concord. A young girl had committed suicide by drowning in the Concord River a few years previously. Perhaps her desperate example rose before Louisa as she stood, in a state of heart-frozen despair, looking down at the swiftly flowing waters of the mill-brook beneath her. The hopelessness in her heart had lasted too long; no relief had come from without and she had not, with the best of intentions, been able to help herself. It occurred to her with an unendurable rush of suffering that she might always be going to feel like this. Anything was better; unconsciousness, dissolution, nothingness would be blessed relief. The despairing mood had only an instant's existence. " It was but a momentary impulse," says her biographer, Mrs. Cheney. But it was a moment to leave a bad scar on the memory. If Louisa, who lived a great deal in her books, had not been able to rehearse and reconquer the temptation of that moment in a scene in a novel, the memory might have left a worse scar.

Lonely but recovering her determined self, Louisa walked on, under the yellowing Concord elms, back to reality. She went back to Boston. There was one resource left. The city buzzed a great deal in those days about the spectacular preacher Theodore Parker. Of pure New England lineage, Parker had abandoned the orthodox church and held a large congregation together by force of his strong personality and challenging eloquence. His fame was just then at its height. He preached, like a true reformer, against corruption, greed, and slavery in all forms. He was the Savonarola of Boston. People flocked to hear him, terrified but fascinated by his exhibition of courage. It was typical of Louisa's friendlessness that she turned for help in her crisis to a public reformer like Parker. He was her last resource, and the great man did not fail her. He gave her a philosophy of life which was timed to her needs, and extended to her his personal friendship.

Dragging herself, almost mechanically, out of her suicidal mood, Louisa went the following Sunday morning to hear Parker preach. As it chanced, he preached that morning about the woman problem. " Laborious

Young Women " was his theme. Parker's church had a social-service department with a social worker in charge. For this reason he knew a great deal about conditions among the working women of the city and was through this knowledge their well-armed champion. As Louisa listened to him, she thought she heard a new evangel. She had never dreamed that there were so many women in the world with lives like her own. Theodore Parker opened the door for her upon a new world. He gave her a philosophy of spinsterhood, which was for Louisa's temperament the unique consolation. With her idealistic tendencies, she at once saw a new life for herself and went from the church dedicated to it. That day she had found the absorbing interest that she had been looking for.

Under the influence of this one sermon of Theodore Parker's, Louisa Alcott built a whole new house of life. She had got an idea of herself as an old maid and she never lost it again. Beneath her idealized vocation was her personal acceptance of the factual state. She always thought of herself henceforth as an " old maid " and spoke of herself as such. This permanent thought meant a great deal in the shaping of her future, for she was an intellectual who lived by ideas.

4

Nothing breeds success like success; no sooner had Bronson Alcott started a real career as a lecturer than Concord appointed him superintendent of schools. So, in the autumn of 1859, when the New York *Tribune* published its usual list of New England lecturers who were "willing" to make engagements in the West, Amos Bronson Alcott's name did not appear. The prophet was at last appreciated in his own country. Emerson went west that year alone. But he went willingly. His long and weary search for a job for his friend had ended in victory. Alcott was drawing a salary, small but regular, from the taxes of the town to which he had once on principle refused to pay taxes. But the town had forgotten it. The new superintendent was welcomed to his office and allowed a free hand in the schools.

There were about a dozen schools in the Concord township, scattered about at wide distances. The sixty-year-old Bronson Alcott trudged from one school-building to another on his own long legs, for a horse was still beyond his means. Snow, rain, and stormy weather had no terrors for this hale and hearty visitant. When the young inexperienced school-teachers saw Alcott coming, they knew they were in for a little vacation, for the superintendent always took the class from them and taught. His old enthusiasm for teaching and the theory of teaching revived and he wrote a report on his work that was much admired and widely circulated.

Alcott introduced gymnastics into the schools. The children were encouraged to move their arms and legs and bodies about in the sacred schoolroom where they had previously sat all day long huddled on wooden benches. Alcott was still the pioneer. But the town now approved of him. The grown-ups bought dumb-bells and organized gymnastic classes in imitation of the school-children. The first year ended with a character-istic Alcott touch. " We spend much on our cattle and flower-shows," said the new superintendent; " let us each Spring have a show of our children, and begrudge nothing for their culture." So the Puritan town of Con-cord had its gymnastics and May Festival and became a pleasanter place under the régime of the youthful-hearted Alcott.

All of his innovations were tolerantly received. His six years as superintendent were without excitement or crisis of any kind. When, at the end of the Civil War, the new country was opened up and beckoned so spec-tacularly, Alcott could not resist the call. Once more he joined the westering flock and left Concord regularly every fall to carry culture far and wide throughout the new land. Cleveland, Cincinnati, and St. Louis all knew Alcott very well in the seventies. He went far-ther and farther from year to year, this son of Spindle Hill, who had from birth that curious element in the blood which drives one restlessly from home out to see the world.

Alcott never earned great sums at lecturing. The year after the Civil War he brought home two hundred dollars. As no records exist to the contrary, he must have earned more afterwards. He was a hard worker at his trade and stuck to it steadily, when many men would have been sitting quietly in their armchairs. His chance came to him late, but he followed it faithfully when it came and made a great success of his career for the last thirty years of his life. It was too late, however, to alter the romantic tradition of the ne'er-do-well, who dreamed and philosophized his time away while his family lived in poverty. This was the Boston tradition and it survived in spite of the friends and partisans that his lecturing made for him in the West.

5

Louisa's life showed almost startlingly the effect of her father's changed fortunes. Soon after he had been made superintendent, she wrote in her diary: " Though in many people's eyes Father may seem improvident, selfish, and indolent — though he often does in my own and I wish he were more like other men — yet I begin to see the purpose of his life and love him for the patient persistence with which he has done what he thought right through all opposition and reproach, for that is what few do I find."

Leaving her lodgings in Boston, she went home to live with her parents in Concord. Orchard House, purchased with her mother's money and renovated by her father's labours, was then very much as it is now — a pleasant, cosy place with arched fireplaces and quaint old furniture. Louisa wrote: " All seem glad that the wandering family is anchored at last. We won't move again for twenty years if I can help it." As it turned out, it was just that long before the family moved again. Meantime, in the spring of 1860, Louisa also settled down to live at Orchard House.

For the first time in her life she was a sheltered and protected woman. She sewed, but she no longer hemmed sheets and pillow-cases. She made a wardrobe for her graceful younger sister, including a ball-dress and a riding-habit, all in the latest fashion. She made a riding-habit for herself; and bought, paid for, and made for herself a new silk dress. Not that she did not wear old clothes; she wore all the old things that Anna and her younger sister, who had gone away to teach, had left at home. But this, too, was a kind of luxury, for it meant that she did not have to present herself suitably garbed as a governess " in the houses of the rich and great." All this gave her a feeling of feminine self-expression such as she had never before experienced.

Louisa's room was on the second floor of Orchard House, but she wrote in the attic. One end of the long bare attic space was partitioned off, whether for her special use or whether it was just so, one does not know. One would like to believe that Bronson Alcott did it for her, but it has not the fine earmarks of his work. The attic chamber is roughly finished. Louisa dragged into it an old sofa and one or two needed articles of furniture. Her æsthetic requirements were of the simplest. Oddly enough, however, she liked to dress herself specially for writing, in a gown and cap. She probably wiped her pen on her gown, for she was not very tidy, and her cap was merely a jaunty touch in millinery. When the late western sun shone into the large window, it fell on a tall figure in a red and green party-wrap and a red and green mob-cap, filling copy-book after copy-book with fine legible writing.

She was writing stories now for the *Atlantic Monthly*. Louisa seldom dared to brave the editorial office of James Russell Lowell, the editor and one of the literary elders of Boston. Her father, coming to her rescue, usually carried her manuscripts to Lowell and did the interviewing for her. As her stories appeared in the *Atlantic,* she began to lay great plans. This daughter of Boston was as delighted with her new magazine as if she had been a child of Kansas. " People seem to think it a great thing to get into the ' Atlantic,' " she said; " but I've not been pegging away all these years in vain, and may yet have books and publishers and a fortune of my own." As she wrote more and more for this monthly, she wrote less and less for the weekly papers. She had taken a step upward in the literary scale, for not only had she acquired a better trade-mark for her work, but she had laid aside her anonymity. She was evolving into a recognized author.

Her reputation gave her self-confidence. An item in her reputation had been her plays, one of which had been produced at a small theatre and another of which had been accepted by a large theatre — and not produced. Still, this very limited amount of success as a playwright had helped to make her name known. Wherever Louisa went now she was regarded as a literary personage and mildly lionized.

Pleasantly spurred on by these acquirements — leisure, a measure of freedom from economic worry, and reputation — she felt the time had come to do what she had long wanted to do — write a novel. So, donning her red and green cloak and cap and seizing her pen, she projected and wrote, in the shortest possible space of time, *Moods,* her first long romance.

The book she had planned for years was completed. Louisa May Alcott, the child of her own ideals, had produced her first novel. It was a very long novel indeed and was dedicated to her mother.

CHAPTER VII

The Civil War

THOUGH the Civil War seemed to burst like an explosion, the war clouds had been gathering for a long time. Premonitions and symptoms of the strife to come had been evident on many hands and in many forms. A phrase from a popular poem, " the irrepressible conflict," had come to be a stock expression and a stock point of view long before the war broke forth, expressing fatalistically what had come to be regarded as inevitable. The public trembled at the stubborn approach of an event which one could neither prevent nor postpone.

The warning clouds hung with especial heaviness over Concord. The town's connection with John Brown, one of the great factors in the conflict, was close and intimate. The Kansas hero had come to the Massachusetts village in the year 1856 and had made connections there through Frank B. Sanborn, who also came from Kansas, and later also through Bronson Alcott, who happened to have been born in Connecticut not far from John Brown's birthplace. But over and above such local ties was the burning ideal which united them. White-hot abolitionists as they were, Sanborn and Alcott were parties in an active sense to John Brown's attack on Harper's Ferry. Quiet little Concord was implicated in this terrible prelude to the great disaster.

In the spring that preceded it, John Brown paid his last visit to his friends in the retired village. Abolition feeling ran high and he was allowed to speak in the Town Hall; the Concordians flocked through the pleasant streets in the sweet May evening to hear him. Bronson Alcott noted: " Our best people listened to his words, — Emerson, Thoreau, Judge Hoar, my wife." Rifles were secretly given him, and funds collected, which he spent for revolutionary pikes in Collinsville, Connecticut, where such implements are still forged. The money went through Alcott's hands, and it is not a little amusing to find the impecunious Alcott figuring in John Brown's notes as his financial patron. The Concord group was completely under the Kansan's spell and regarded him as another Danton. While they shuddered at his plans, to which — says Sanborn — they " gave their reluctant consent," " they avoided " — adds Alcott — " asking particulars." Alcott and his friends were parties to the Harper's Ferry rising.

When the news of John Brown's capture came back in the fall, it had a bitter tang for these allies. His failure awakened a painful and apprehensive echo. Yet at the hour of his execution Alcott, Sanborn, Emerson, and others forgathered in the Town Hall, where he had spoken in the spring, and held a memorial service. To the sighing accompaniment of a little organ they had carried in for the purpose, hymns for the dying were sung and Alcott read the service for the death of a martyr. Thoreau spoke, and so did Emerson. Still sentiment was so divided in the little town that the selectmen would not allow the bell to be tolled.

Louisa was living at Orchard House while these events were taking place, and watched the uprising through to its tragic conclusion. " I am glad I have lived to see the anti-slavery movement," she said, " and this last heroic act in it." Alas, it was not the last, but merely the first, the fatal beginning! But she did not go to the memorial meeting in the Town Hall for the surprisingly trivial reason that she had no " good gown." She may have been somewhat terrified at the possible outcome of the gathering at such a time, for Louisa was no fighting revolutionist. She stayed at home that day and, noticing an indoor rose which had bloomed that fateful morn, wrote a poem to the rose and to the

> . . . moment when the brave old man,
>   Went so serenely forth,
> With foot-steps whose unfaltering tread
>   Re-echoed through the North.

It was but an indifferent pæan, — Louisa said of it afterwards: " I am a better patriot than poet " — and it was deservedly lost among hundreds of others on the same subject published in the *Liberator*.

2

When the war actually came, Louisa tried picking lint and rolling bandages with the other women, but she did not like it. Her idea of herself as an " old maid," to which she had strenuously schooled herself, would have been useful now, had it not fallen away and her old adventurous self come back. The tall young woman, who wore no hoop-skirts when other women did, attracted no masculine attention, and could walk twenty miles without tiring, seemed more like one of the soldiers than like one of the sisters, wives, and mothers of the Concord company. When she went to the station to see the " boys " off, she wished ever so strongly that she could go with them. " I've often longed to see a war," she said, " and now I have my wish. I long to be a man."

During the first year of the Civil War, Louisa paid no very great attention to it. On the contrary, she wrote her first novel, *Moods* — a two-volume masterpiece — and triumphantly finished it. Then she tried to get it published. By this time the war was in full swing — the war of which Henry James said that it was " not a cheerful time for any persons but armycontractors " — and Louisa was now willy-nilly forced

ORCHARD HOUSE

Courtesy of the Louisa M. Alcott Association

to pay attention to it. Her novel went from publisher to publisher and finally came back to lie on the shelf, a dusty memorial to the fact that the Civil War was raging. When veteran novelists like Hawthorne were on the verge of starvation, what could a recruit like Louisa hope for? She had chosen the most unfortunate moment possible to try to publish a first novel. Poor inexperienced Louisa! She sank into bewilderment and discouragement, and fell back on writing for the cheap weekly papers which she now deplored.

The first escape from this that offered was teaching in one of the new kindergartens. Elizabeth Peabody, faithful to her life's aim of reforming education, was introducing the Froebel system in Boston in spite of the great conflict. Miss Peabody urged Louisa to take charge of one of the new kindergarten classes. For one winter Louisa did — " a wasted winter," she said later. In despair she fled from the experiment before it was over, leaving her sister May and Miss Peabody to clear away the remnants of her mis-spent activities.

Back to Concord and her writing sped Louisa. She closed her door on the rising waves of war-passion which beat against it from the outside and sat down to her own occupation. She was determined to write stories again; and these not for the low-brow weeklies but for the highly respected *Atlantic*. She wrote one. By her father, she sent it to the new editor, James T. Fields. Moved by one knows not what perverse impulse in a world full of perverse impulses, Fields not only rejected Louisa's manuscript but added a gratuitous word of advice. " Tell Louisa," he said to her father, " to stick to her teaching. She can never write." This was the worst of the many blows that came to Louisa in that first year of the war.

Though she pretended to be defiant, she did not feel so. The accumulation of disappointments and failures had worn her down to the grain at last. She had started a second novel, but while her beloved first-born still accumulated dust on the shelf, she could not finish another. There was nothing left for her to do but to go on rolling bandages and picking lint in Concord. Though she scarcely knew what had caused it, she knew that her talent and career had been cut off. Wherever she looked around her, she saw nothing but the war.

3

No help was to be had from her sister Anna. Nan had got married just when war was declared. In the midst of Lincoln's first call for troops, as innocent as Louisa concerning all that this might mean, Anna had stepped off, and had gone to live on the other side of Boston — specifically, Chelsea. For a year the grim war rolled on over her unconscious wifely head. Like Louisa, she paid no very great attention to the problems it brought at first.

Her Chelsea paradise seemed only to be touched by the hard times. The common necessities of life had risen to an unheard-of cost, and mere housekeeping was a heroic occupation. The idyll in the Chelsea cottage would have been less complete — more damaged, in short — by having to make both ends meet, if Anna and her husband had not both been brought up on the simple life of Concord. But spiritual problems rose up to harass them. The enlistment campaign increased its pressure and finally called upon the women for help. In the end conscription came, later than it had in the South, and was when it came actually a relief from the former stress and strain. In the meantime every wife of every able-bodied husband had lived through torturous days and nights, whatever the final solution in her own husband's case. Anna's husband did not join the army in spite of the stress and strain, but he had to endure much.

Louisa's problem was a long way off from her sister's. She was trying to occupy herself with doing nothing in Concord. She plunged into reading, choosing heroic books like Carlyle's *French Revolution* and the *Life of Sir Thomas More,* works in keeping with the moral atmosphere of the Civil War. She made a critical study of the early English novels. But history and criticism could not occupy Louisa long nor strike any live sparks from her. A month's vacation in the White Mountains, whither she loved enormously to go, helped to pass the time; but that, too, came to an end. In the autumn she returned to Concord, once more empty-handed and with empty days before her.

On her return from the White Mountains, she heard

great news from Anna — news that was like a trumpet-
call to her starved and deafened emotions. Anna was
going to have a baby. Anna's life was going on in spite
of mountainous obstacles. Louisa decided that her own
course had run in the sands long enough: it was time
that it found some swifter way of flowing. She found a
way within a month. She wrote to Washington and vol-
unteered to go to the war as an army nurse.

4

The pioneer example of Florence Nightingale in the
Crimean War was vivid in the public mind at the time,
her notes on nursing having just been published. Another pioneer army nurse, born not many miles from
Louisa's home and later the founder of the American
Red Cross — Clara Barton — had been at the Civil
War front for more than a year. For Louisa's imagination, fixed on a life of striving, these heroic women had
great meaning. Her decision to go to the war stirred
Concord to its depths. "Great events are thickening
here," wrote Mrs. Hawthorne to her family, apropos of
Louisa's volunteering. Bronson Alcott's remark to all
and sundry was that he was sending his only son to the
war. Louisa was going to play the man's part in this too
feminine family.

It was on a day of cold wet thaw that she left for
Washington. She spent the day in Boston, leaping on
long legs over one mud-puddle after the other, trying to

find someone to give her a pass for the journey. The Alcotts never paid railroad fare if they could help it. At last, exhausted but successful, she seated herself breathless at twilight in the train headed for New London. From New London to Jersey City was a night's boat-trip; and in the early grey sooty dawn of the day following she clambered into the train that would take her to Washington.

The trip was for Louisa, who had virtually never seen the world outside of Concord and Boston, a strange and wonderful progress. Passing through Philadelphia, she peered curiously out at her native city. "Everyone seems to be scrubbing their white steps. All the houses look like tidy jails, with their outside shutters." Speeding through Maryland, that long-lost paradise of her father's youth, she thought it disappointing, with its " dreary little houses, with chimneys built outside, with clay and rough sticks piled crosswise, as we used to build cob-towers." The sight that pleased her most was the Southern mule, " an odd beast . . . with small feet, a nicely trimmed tassel of a tail, perked up ears . . ." and an almost human character, as Louisa was convinced by observing him. The coloured people astonished her most, " looking as if they had come out of a picture-book, or off the stage, but not at all like the sort of people I'd been accustomed to see at the North."

She reached Washington after dark, and her first

glimpse of the White House was of a shining mansion
" all lighted up." On out through the darkness of evening she drove to Georgetown, and stopped at last before a great rambling building with flags flying over it
and sentinels standing at the door. It was the Union
Hotel Hospital, to which she had been assigned as a
nurse.

5

Louisa's hospital was probably neither worse nor better than the average botched-up institution of the kind
during the Civil War. It was apparently about as good
as the one in which Walt Whitman served. The only
difference was that the Georgetown hospital had formerly been a hotel and had some suggestion of former
comfortable living in its fireplaces, living-rooms, and
outlying stables, while the other was merely a barracks.
But this suggestion of domesticity only led Louisa all
the more to contrast it with households she had known
in New England. The Union Hotel Hospital, poor
enough in its appointments, was made to seem like a
hovel in her eyes by her comparisons. She was ill prepared by her orderly New England life to endure the
crowding, the confusion, and the general hit-or-miss-
ness. In short, the hastily invoked and chaotic institution would have been an ordeal for anyone, and par-
ticularly for one who had been brought up, like Louisa,
in a quiet and cleanly physical environment.

She had come a long way to this place. Neither

Louisa nor any other distant Concordian could have realized its nature in advance. " Louisa is determined to make the soldiers jolly," Mrs. Hawthorne had written her family from Concord, "and takes all of Dickens that she has, and games." But during the hours of Louisa's journey hither, the battle of Fredericksburg had been raging; and when the new nurse arrived at the door of the hospital the wounded from that battle were being driven up in vanloads. During her first hour on duty, a stricken man died under her ministrations. It was the beginning of a day of horrors. There was small need for Dickens and for games in that hospital after Fredericksburg had done its work. Yet Louisa *did* use her Dickens in one case, reeling off pages and pages of *David Copperfield* from memory to a man who was having his arm taken off without ether.

Scarcely more than twenty-four hours from Orchard House, she was plunged into this, an untried, untrained, and undisciplined novice. Soldiers were put through a minimum of training, but nurses were sent straightway into this inferno. It is impossible to conceive of a greater shock to a sensitive nature and an emotional type. In spite of her thirty years, Louisa confessed that she was " ignorant, awkward, and bashful in a new and trying situation." The inconveniences and discomforts of the physical and social life would have been hard enough for her to bear without the added responsibility of the doomed creatures around her.

She was man-shy in the extreme. At her first view of

the hospital she had exclaimed with alarm when she saw the number of whole, healthy men who were standing about. What she had expected of the patients of an army hospital would be hard to guess; certainly she had not the least idea of what flesh-and-blood men, sick and suffering at that, were like. Her sexual inhibitions made some of the simplest duties she had to perform into heroic services. Sex, pain, and death crowded upon her senses incessantly day and night, while she was near to sinking from fatigue and sleeplessness. The pity of such things could find expression for Louisa only through her imagination, and her imagination was cut off through the life of service she was trying to live.

The end was that she became a patient herself. The doctors put her to bed when symptoms of typhoid and pneumonia appeared. The swift telegraph carried a message through from Washington to Concord. Promptly in response to it the faithful, grey-haired father, always the traveller and first-aid in misfortune, came flying to the rescue. He piloted her somehow without assistance all the way back to Orchard House, to her own bed and upstairs chamber. There she lay for three weeks, with a raging temperature and fevered visions. "The most vivid and enduring was the conviction that I had married a stout, handsome Spaniard, dressed in black velvet, with very soft hands, and a voice that was continually saying, 'Lie still, my dear!' This was Mother, I suspect; and with all the comfort I often found in her presence, there was blended an awful fear of the Spanish spouse who was always coming after me, appearing out of closets, in at windows, or threatening me dreadfully all night long. I appealed to the Pope, and really got up and made a touching plea in something meant for Latin, they tell me. Once I went to heaven, and found it a twilight place, with people darting through the air in a queer way, — all very busy, and dismal, and ordinary." Another vision remembered was of " tending millions of rich men who never died or got well." She emerged from these weeks of illness, and more weeks of tedious convalescence, with most of her long, abundant hair gone and a permanent crack in her health which was like the hair-line across a valuable piece of china. It never rings quite the same afterwards.

This was Louisa's whole reward for her war services. The war had done as much to her in four weeks as it had done in four years to some others. " She was one of the veterans of the Civil War," said one of the most understanding students of Louisa's personality, Frank P. Stearns of Boston, " and deserved a pension." She did not get it. All that she got was experience, ten dollars, and the right to wear a curly wig.

6

Louisa's youngest sister, Abbie, was growing up to imitate her own height. But Abbie was also graceful, with a mass of wavy golden hair instead of Louisa's dark chestnut. She was not more beautiful otherwise, however, than her sister. Yet she had the knack of looking picturesque; and when she dashed about the Concord roads on horseback, accompanied by Louisa, it was she who was mostly seen, admired, and remembered.

Abbie was growing up conventional — her reaction to Louisa's brusqueness. Her respect for the proprieties was her answer to Louisa's scorn of them. She was misled into an occasional preciousness in words and manners which stirred Louisa to uproarious hilarity — which in turn led Abbie to more preciousness. Her love of the fleshpots, starting in a childhood of spoiling, was something that was entirely her own and something that she never entirely outgrew.

Abbie Alcott had early decided that " Abbie " was too plain a name for her and had whisked it into " May." " May Alcott " she was henceforth to the world and her family. As May Alcott she commenced as early as Louisa to carve out a career for herself. Her opportunity came in the form of education known as " finishing." The benignant Boston aunts, who still kept a watchful eye on Mrs. Alcott's fortunes, observed that her youngest daughter showed signs of developing into a conventional young lady. Thereupon one of them invited May to spend a winter in her house and paid for her lessons in French, music, and drawing. The plain Concord family, including Louisa, was delighted that May was to be " finished." " If her eyes hold out," wrote Louisa to Bronson, then lecturing in New York, " she will . . . become what none of us can

LOUISA MAY ALCOTT

*from a photograph made about 1862
Courtesy of Little, Brown and Company*

be, ' an accomplished Alcott.' " Deep in her heart, Louisa respected May's methods because she saw that they worked.

But no child of Bronson Alcott could remain an amateur. Whatever may be said of his theory of education, his practice was effective on his children. May developed under her finished régime a serious love of art and soon busied herself devotedly with her new occupation. She tried sculpture, painting, drawing; according to whichever tools came handiest, she applied herself to that art. She ornamented the doors and window-frames of her room at Orchard House, and they still bear witness to her overwhelming passion, in a series of decorative outline drawings. Her own foot, done in plaster, also survives there as a memento of the ardent young sculptor. Some of her early pencil sketches of her Concord environment were later published, showing that May was never by way of becoming merely " an accomplished Alcott." She was an earnest art student from the first. It was her father's hand that led her into this path; Louisa had no concept of art as a visual experience — she was so passionately literary.

As it happened, Boston was no mean art centre in the days just before the Civil War. Its culture had reached a sort of golden age, just before the war clouds broke, which it had never before and has never since attained. A new School of Design had been opened; William Morris Hunt, who had returned from Fontainebleau, taught painting, and Dr. William Rimmer, more distinguished than Hunt in those days, taught sculpture and drawing. Through gifts of money from her aunts and her own strenuous efforts May was able to work herself up into these studios and had instruction comparable to the best instruction abroad. She attended Hunt's life-classes and studied anatomical drawing with Rimmer. At the age of eighteen she taught classes in Concord and sold drawings; then she taught classes in Boston and studied again. There was the same note in May which appeared so early in Louisa — a professional note which lifted her out of the antimacassar class and into the ranks of the real artists.

Louisa watched her sister's strides with mixed feelings. Though always proud of May, she did not appreciate her ability. The character of Amy in *Little Women* does not do justice to the personality of the original — if fiction may be expected to do justice. This fictionized May was the obverse of her feelings; the reverse is seen when other sponsors failed and Louisa stepped into the breach with her own hard-earned dollars and enabled her sister to continue with her excellent masters. She soon had dreams of sending May to Italy, representing to her literary mind the ultima Thule of artists. May could probably have told her then, but did not, that her destination was Paris.

Louisa's protection of May was elder-sisterly and loyal rather than spontaneous and affectionate; for Louisa seemed to have buried the soft side of her nature in the grave of her sister Betty. But she was intensely proud of this youngest specimen of the " Alcott brains " and strong in her belief in her.

7

Two more years of Civil War remained after Louisa's illness. Contrary to what might have been expected, they proved one of the more peaceful periods of Alcott family history. While almost everyone was on the verge of bankruptcy, except a few war-mongers, this exceptional family lived in an oasis of comparative security. As long as Bronson Alcott's position as superintendent of schools lasted, it kept the wolf from the door. Louisa lived at home and wrote without hiring a furnished room in Boston. May commuted to the city like a modern business woman. Orchard House grew mellow and comfortable with use — became a genuine home. It was another halcyon period like the early one at Hillside.

But still Louisa's *Moods* was not published. Just after Lincoln's re-election she dusted off the manuscript again and submitted it through a friend's kind offices to yet another publisher. Promptly an astonishing thing happened. The publisher said that he would take the book, bring it out at once. The event could be only the harbinger of a great change. People were in fact beginning to feel obscurely that the war might one day come to an end. Publishers were beginning to take risks and accept manuscripts again. The sour mood in which Fields had told Louisa she could never write had yielded to a more hopeful one generally and Fields himself would hardly have sent her this message at this time. Louisa's novel was about to see the light because the North felt that there was going to be peace.

When that glad day finally came, Louisa donned her bonnet and shawl and took the cars for Boston. She wanted to immerse herself in the thick of the gaiety that overflowed the city. A mad carnival was in progress; the population of Boston poured forth in every kind of burlesque and masquerade to celebrate the victory. Tall and sombre-eyed, Louisa followed the wild procession, her solitary, separate soul for one day merged and mingled with the soul of the multitude.

8

The terrible war was over. The four black years were behind. But they had left their dark impression on the whole country. Concord, though far from the actual conflict, had not escaped their destructive path. Thoreau was dead; Hawthorne was dead; transcendentalism was dead. Henceforth life in the old village would flow in new grooves and channels.

Louisa Alcott's first novel, written in one world, would be read in another. Anna Alcott's children, born on the verge of its discovery, would be residents of a new continent. May Alcott's maturity would be separated by æons from her youth. She belonged to a generation who would have to make and live by their own patterns. Life would never be the same again in the United States.

All this was to affect Louisa May Alcott's eventual future profoundly. But first circumstances were to intervene that were to postpone her entrance on the new scene for another year.

CHAPTER VIII

Love

IN the heyday of New England, people considered it proper for every ambitous young man and young woman to complete the grand tour. Able but impecunious young men went to Europe on cattle-boats; young women, as travelling companions. The opportunity was bound to come to the ambitious sooner or later, and it came to Louisa immediately after peace was declared.

No sooner had the smoke of battle cleared away than the relieved and comfortable classes of New England began to assemble their travelling bags and passports. Every Cunard liner that left Boston harbour in the summer of 1865 was loaded with war-weary Americans bent on a holiday. The general exodus increased the demand for travelling companions. Within a month

Louisa had two invitations to go abroad with all her expenses paid.

Her novel had done this much for her if it had done nothing else. It had established her not only as ambitious but as on the road to fame. The approval of Henry James, Senior, was her best recommendation. The elder James, crack lion-tamer of the period, had met Louisa in her father's company and had pointedly invited the daughter without the father to dine. James wasted no ammuniton on those whom he considered sheep. "Met Henry James, Senior," Louisa noted, " and he asked me to come and dine. Also called upon me with Mrs. James. I went, and was treated like the Queen of Sheba." The author of a season's novel, a book of popular sketches, and of many well-known short stories, Louisa was more of a public figure than she realized. The Jameses' invitation, had she known it, was a kind of accolade.

Louisa's first chance to go to Europe came to her at her sister Anna's house in Chelsea. While visiting Anna and her week-old baby, she met an affluent friend of the family bent on the same quest. Out of the blue this lady asked her to go to Europe with her sister. Louisa answered with a diffident " yes "; " but as I spoke neither French nor German, she didn't think I'd do." So the opportunity was lost. But shortly afterwards, in fact within the following week, a Mr. Weld of Boston gave her another chance. Mr. Weld's proposition was that she should accompany his invalid daughter, who was taking the trip for her health. Louisa, who was a nurse only in her imagination, though she still cherished the idea that she was a nurse in fact, responded to this invitation with more enthusiasm. Nevertheless she demurred for a week before accepting the proffered post. She only decided at last on the eve of sailing.

Miss Anna Weld was the lady whose health gave Louisa this opportunity. If we may risk an informal diagnosis, she was not seriously ill, her ailment being of the kind for which a European tour is prescribed. We are not surprised, then, to find her later holding out well as a traveller, at times better than her nurse. She stood the ocean voyage as well as Louisa and was not more delighted to set her feet again on solid earth. The trip which followed, beginning at Liverpool and extending through London, Dover, Brussels, Cologne, Wiesbaden, Frankfurt, Heidelberg, and Switzerland, all taken at a breakneck tourist pace except for a pause at Schwalbach, would have shaken a really delicate constitution to bits. But Miss Weld's health stood the strain and she arrived at Lake Geneva on their tour reasonably whole and fit. The duties of the nurse had not been heavy.

Louisa was constantly in an excited so-this-is-Europe state of mind. Each carved statue, tiled roof, beautiful view set her blood pounding; each historical memory made her pulse beat faster. The journey was the magical fulfilment of a lifelong dream. She was untiring as long as it continued; it was only in the occasional pauses, as at Schwalbach, that she found her duties as companion too arduous. But travel, not pause, was the order of the day and both she and Miss Weld seemed to prefer it so; the journey started off under the most hopeful auspices.

2

Arriving at Vevey in the middle of October, they settled down for one of their brief stops. The terraces bright with flowers, the azure water, and the black and white peaks beyond the lake made the place one of the most bewitching spots Louisa had seen. The pension, kept by an Englishwoman, was no strain on her linguistic limitations and was comfortable and pleasant. But after a few days she found the place irksome. " I did not enjoy the life nor the society after the first novelty wore off, for I missed my freedom and grew . . . tired of the daily worry. . . ." The dreamy charm and beauty of the landscape were not enough to keep Louisa's active imagination occupied.

In this mood she came down to breakfast one morning to find a new guest seated at the table. The new guest was a tall dark-eyed young man — not unlike herself in the part of Roderigo. He was thin and pale, however, and only his vivid smile and lively manners contradicted his appearance of illness. Louisa observed that he coughed frequently, especially when a door was opened near him, and she concluded that the draught was bad for him. With all her old hospital habits, she rushed to the rescue. Sending word through her landlady that she would exchange seats with the new guest, she chivalrously took charge of him. The young man responded gallantly and amenably and so the acquaintance began.

Vevey was no longer the same place for Louisa. The outlook was charming, the terraces lovely, the season glorious. The lake was inviting, the pension homelike, the guests entertaining. The arrival of the stranger had made everything different, as colours grow strong in Japanese paper flowers that have been placed in water. Louisa was surprised herself at the sudden change in her spirits. One day when the wind blew, as it sometimes did even in Vevey, driving the autumn clouds and making a variegated landscape, she remarked in her diary: " The day is very like me in its fitful changes of sunshine and shade."

Ladislas Wisniewski was a young Polish musician. The legend has tried to make this friend of Louisa's, like his countryman Chopin, into a famous pianist. Ladislas played the piano well enough to give music lessons, to entertain the guests at the pension, and to perform duets, to Louisa's annoyance, with Madame Teiblin, the other musician of the pension. But he was no genius nor in the same class with George Sand's great beloved. He resembled Chopin merely in being a Pole, tubercular, and the favourite of a famous woman author. Though Ladislas was a charming, brilliant, and versatile young man, neither history nor biography would take much account of him but for his association with Louisa.

Ladislas's dark eyes and general delicacy recalled the lost and forgotten " brown boy," William Lane. But he was unlike the nut-brown William in being vivacious and merry. This was the way the serious-eyed Louisa felt inwardly. Ladislas revealed to her his serious side and she to him her merry side, and this mutual recognition was the basis of a delightful comradeship. They spent their days together, exchanging lessons in English and French, rowing on the broad blue lake, and taking long walks in the marvellous weather. They had long confidential talks, which sometimes extended on into the evening if Ladislas did not happen to play for the other guests. Thus the autumn days slid by in quick succession and grew into the swift weeks, while no complaints of the irksome stay emanated from Louisa.

There was a difference in age between them of thirteen or fourteen years. But the difference seemed less by reason of a deceptive maturity in Ladislas. By comparison with the youths of nineteen or twenty whom she had known in Concord and among the Western pupils of Sanborn's school, this Polish youth seemed a highly finished product. It was her first encounter with that precocity of manners in the European male which to the average American female is so misleading. The European who can bow like a veteran, speak several languages, and produce formal behaviour for all sorts of occasions was an incredible type to Louisa. That Ladislas was somewhat taller than herself — something she rarely met with in his sex — confirmed her illusion of his maturity. The philosophy which he brought to bear on his illness was also a rare attainment for one so young. Even if the tall young Pole had not responded to her care of him by showing a protecting and helpful attitude toward herself, Louisa would still have thought of him as many years older than he was.

Both of them had been through wars. Ladislas Wisniewski had taken part in the Polish nationalist uprising of 1863, the same year in which Louisa had served in the army hospital. He was in exile for his principles. Revolutionary feeling ran high in him. At the sight of a Russian baron who bobbed up in Vevey with his family, Ladislas flew into a great passion, and Louisa was equally enraged at the sight of a Virginia colonel and his family. They hated tyrants together. The revolutionary feeling grew less strong in them as their friendship developed, but other ties grew up among the grapes, flowers, and sunshine of Vevey.

Thus two gracious, joyous months were passed. The absence of Miss Weld from the chronicles of this life is noted, but nothing more positive than absence is shown. In December, Miss Weld reappears in the chronicle, as she and her companion prepared to go on with their itinerary. They assembled their effects and made ready to depart. At the last moment there was some delay owing to fear of the cholera in Nice; but they left Vevey finally on the 6th of December, accompanied by Ladislas. At Lausanne their escort saw that all their bags and shawls were in place, kissed their hands in courtly farewell, and stood on the platform waving to them as their train moved away. It was not to be a long farewell, however, for there was the prospect of a reunion in Paris in the spring. Though a tear or two fell at parting, the occasion was not as painful as it would otherwise have been.

3

Louisa's passion for roses was gratified in Nice. The sight of whole villas buried in them stirred her as did few things in the visible world. In the forest of Var she strolled among acres of blooming daisies. The grandeur of the palms and the ilexes entranced her less than these homely plants flowering lusciously in midwinter. " With friends, health, and a little money," she wrote in her diary, " how jolly one might be in this perpetual summer."

Something more than usual was wrong with Louisa. It was Miss Weld: her reaction to Nice had been instantaneous and unhappy. She had taken to her bed at once, had called in a doctor, and had appealed to the American consul. On New Year's Day she was too ill to receive as one did in Boston, and Louisa, with her slenderly developed social resources, was obliged to reproduce the Boston New Year's Day alone. As Miss

Weld then grew no better, it was decided to hire an apartment and a maid and to set about keeping house. With the doctor's and the consul's assistance, Miss Weld secured an elegantly furnished six-room flat at No. 10 rue Geoffredo and hired a Frenchwoman as cook and housekeeper. Here she and Louisa were installed within a fortnight after arriving in Nice.

Whether Louisa might have prevented this step is hard to say. Once it was taken, the complications for her were serious. Life in the apartment was pleasant enough: for the first time in her existence she knew what it meant to lead a life of comfort and ease — to be waited on and fed delightfully as a matter of routine. But Miss Weld's health did not improve under the new régime. The doctor was in regular attendance and the nurse's services were in steady request. Louisa was a prisoner. Things went on thus from week to week and from month to month. The winter passed. Spring approached, with the pair of travellers still in Nice; while Italy and Rome, where they were to have spent the winter, had receded farther and farther into the distance.

It is impossible not to see in these semi-tragic events the human drama of Miss Weld's revenge. Supported by a physician and the American consul, she was probably compensating herself for past neglect. She had apparently fallen back on her two certainties: bad health and money. Louisa was in bondage to both. Miss Weld simply dug in comfortably in Nice and refused to go farther. With regular visits from her physician, calls from the American consul, and the skilful services of her housekeeper, she was not at all bored. Occasionally she saw Americans from home who stopped in Nice on their way to Rome. She was the typical nervous invalid: tyrannical, suffering, incurable. Enthroned in her elegant French bed, she ruled her environment by her pains. Rarely she drove out in an easy carriage; once only did she venture forth in a wheeled chair, with a man to propel her, and Louisa to entertain her. But most of the time she just escaped serious illness without making any progress toward serious recovery. Above all, her suffering was made endurable by the sure knowledge that there was plenty of money to sustain her in whatever state she remained and for as long a time as was necessary. The point was that as long as she did not go to Italy they could not go on to Paris, where the reunion with Ladislas was scheduled to take place. Miss Weld's condition remained just the same.

On her first arrival at the rue Geoffredo flat, Louisa was apparently overcome by premonitions. " Couldn't sleep at all for some nights, and felt very poorly, for my life didn't suit me and the air was too exciting." Still, if she was a prisoner, she could have been a prisoner in a worse place. Nice was a popular winter resort. The crowds on the Promenade des Anglais rivalled the turn-out on the Nevsky Prospect and Unter den Linden. There was a first-class theatre, where, even without understanding much French, she could enjoy good plays and fine acting. Adelaide Ristori as Medea and Queen Elizabeth was one of the high-lights of her otherwise dull winter. But nothing could quench her longing for Rome and Paris. With the goal of her desire only a few hours away, she was as helpless to attain it as if it had been the North Pole. Miss Weld would not budge; nothing could move her. Long afterwards Louisa said of this experience: " Now, being a nervous invalid myself, I understand what seemed whims, selfishness, and folly in others " — which was certainly as much charity as Miss Weld deserved.

At last Louisa in desperation gave notice. Not even this could stir Miss Weld from her safe retreat. With the long warning that Louisa's notice had given her, she might still have recovered and continued her journey to Italy with her companion. But no change in her condition took place — no surcease in the dreary nursing befell. Three months more of it was all that Louisa earned by her honest attempt to give Miss Weld time to fill her place.

The only event of importance that took place before she left was the receipt of money for her return. By a miracle her mother had sent her enough to enable her to stay over several weeks in Paris and in London on the way. Though the loss of Italy and Rome was bitter, Louisa's trip was thus more than saved. She would still be able to carry out the planned reunion in Paris and see something of life in London. On the first day of May she stepped on the train with a light heart. Miss

LOUISA MAY ALCOTT

from a photograph made soon after the Civil War

Weld, perhaps equally relieved, remained to finish out her six months' lease in Nice.

4

May-day had always been celebrated by the Alcotts, and the trip to Paris was Louisa's special celebration this year. When her train rolled into the station, Ladislas Wisniewski was waiting on the platform to meet her. With his usual gay spirits he led her to a carriage and drove with her to her pension.

The next day was the beginning of a charming idyll. Ladislas, arrayed in English clothes, with chamois gloves and swinging cane, called early for Louisa at the pension. To match this grandeur, she went forth and bought herself a new hat. They selected it together. It required a great deal of consideration in order that the covering might be neither too gay nor too sober. They finally agreed upon a broad-brimmed affair with a crêpe rose. From that time on, life was one continuous round of pleasure. Their days were spent in sightseeing and excursions: one day it was the Louvre they visited, another day the Musée de Cluny or the Champs-Élysées; other days they went to the environs, to Saint-Cloud or Fontainebleau, for a picnic. Every evening, without fail, Ladislas brought flowers to Louisa at the pension.

They resumed their study of languages. The versatile young Pole had undertaken the ambitious task of translating *Vanity Fair* into his native language; he was turning Becky Sharp into Polish. Every day he brought his worst problems in translation and he and Louisa struggled together to achieve just the right word and the right shade of meaning needed. When they had accomplished some such effort to their satisfaction it was an occasion for delight and hilarity. A gay companionship was theirs without tiresome claims or interruptions from others to trouble it.

But fortune had ironically supplied it with one false note. Ladislas lived with two Polish friends in the Latin Quarter. They, too, were revolutionaries and exiles, and the three friends were like the three mousquetaires, sharing their resources and braving misfortune together. For Louisa this trio of ex-soldiers had no social terrors. She welcomed Ladislas's friends with open arms, rejoiced in their successes, and sympathized with their misfortunes. They were the same " boys " she had known in the army hospital, only marvellously preserved from wounds, amputations, and other marks of battle. She had met them suffering in the ghostly night-watches of the Union Hotel Hospital and lying on ghastly stretchers borne through its echoing hallways. Now she sat with the jolly three, all whole and sound, under the spreading shade of the Luxembourg Gardens, sipping chocolate and listening to the concert.

By their mere presence, however, the two Polish youths were a check on Louisa's romance. When the dream threatened to become altogether too delightful, Porthos and Athos had a way of bobbing up to dissipate it. They were unglamorous duplicates of Aramis, em-

144

phasizing by repetition the differences and obstacles that separated her from their comrade. " Thanks to them," said Louisa, " I discovered a joke played on me by my ' polisson.' He told me to call him ' ma drogha,' saying that it meant ' my friend ' in Polish. . . . Using it one day before the other lads . . . I found to my dismay that I had been calling him ' my darling ' in the tenderest manner. . . . Laddie clasped his hands and begged pardon, explaining that jokes were necessary to his health, and he never meant me to know the full baseness of this ' pleasantrie.' I revenged myself," she added, " by giving him some bad English for his translation and telling him of it just as I left Paris."

But the romance was nevertheless charming. Louisa was no prima donna and Ladislas no gigolo. Louisa was not famous or rich at the time; she was merely to these Europeans the travelling companion of a well-to-do lady. Though thirty-three, she was under the influence of an upwelling biological urge that produces the hallucination of youth in its victim. " My twelve years' seniority," she said primly, " made our adventures quite proper." Ladislas called her " Little Mamma," but he felt toward her as toward a comrade. The lovers' relation between them was real while it lasted. It is impossible to believe that a proposal of marriage in some form did not take place, though Louisa gives no hint of it. The thought of separating forever could only have meant poignant grief on both sides. But whatever the nature of the supreme moment of their relationship was, Louisa does not reveal it, and it passed without leaving any permanent outward change in their lives.

Louisa was more timid about life than most women — more timid about life, but less timid about art. She had already taken too many bold flights into the empyrean of the imagination — had experienced the terror and ecstasy of such flights far too often — to feel about the great adventure of life, when she met it, as if it were the only one. Love had not the same finality for her that it would have had, had she been less of an artist. Saying good-bye that last day at the station in Paris, when a kiss — not on the hand this time — was their last communion, she could still realize that underneath all the pain and sorrow of the moment the possibility of delight was not lost in her soul.

5

On a fair day around the middle of May in 1866, a tall, large-eyed, quickly moving young lady alighted in the London station from the boat-train just in from Dover. The tall lady, Miss Louisa Alcott, was met by a gentleman who spoke with a Southern accent. Mr. Moncure Conway, the gentleman, did not tarry long in London with his guest. He took her at once to his place in the country. A rambling thatched farmhouse, surrounded by white clouds of hawthorne and a yellow sea of gorse, was the home which this American had chosen for himself in England. It was the nearest thing to Ann Hathaway's cottage that he could find.

Her visit of two weeks with the Moncure Conways allowed Louisa to continue her dream without too harsh an awakening. The song of the lark at dawn and the trill of the nightingale by night prolonged the note of beauty that had lately become a part of her life. The feeling of the Old World around her, mellow and peaceful, softened the sharp edges of joy and pain. The memories of Paris only rose before her to become a part of this gentle and forgiving scene.

The place was Wimbledon Common, on the outskirts of London. Louisa's host had been called to London several years since to take charge of a Unitarian congregation. From his country home he made daily journeys to the city and he sometimes took Louisa with him to see the sights. There she met Mr. Peter Taylor, one of the leading radicals and political figures of the day and a member of Mr. Conway's congregation. An invitation from the Taylors to visit them transported her into the midst of London Liberal society — Mr. Taylor, a Member of the House of Commons, being an indefatigable and generous host to his friends. At his house she met the greatest celebrities of the day. She chatted with John Bright, listened to John Stuart Mill make one of his speeches in Parliament, and was introduced to the rising William E. Gladstone. It was a time of great political excitement in the city, when the Liberals and Tories were locked in one of their historic battles. Louisa accommodated herself to the atmosphere of crisis and moved about in it easily, diverted, self-possessed, and interested. A striking symptom of her new sufficiency was her loss of interest in her clothes. She had left home on a week's notice and had bought nothing since except a hat in Paris. But, accustomed to worry about this detail as she was, she forgot entirely to do so while staying with the Taylors in London and " seeing English society."

Her literary contacts were somewhat less brilliant than her political ones. Carlyle, whom she should certainly have met, was living at the moment in deep retirement at Chelsea after his wife's death. Dickens was so famous that she did not dare to approach him nearer than a seat at one of his public readings. But she had tea with Jean Ingelow, whose " High Tide on the Coast of Lincolnshire " was then on everybody's lips, and she made the acquaintance of Mathilde Blind, the Jewish author and suffragist. George Eliot she did not meet, though she stayed within a stone's throw of the novelist's house for several weeks. It is doubtful whether she had or even sought a glimpse of her neighbour. It seems a mistake of fate that two characters who had so much in common should have passed so near each other without speaking. More self-sacrificing spirits than Louisa Alcott and George Eliot have rarely existed or devoted themselves to literature. That both of them looked out of their windows on the same Regent's Park awhile is the only coincidence that can be chronicled — that and the fact that Louisa Alcott once declared she did not admire George Eliot.

After leaving the Taylors, Louisa boarded in a tall, pillared, cream-coloured boarding-house kept by a Mrs. Travers. From this stately, rather cold-looking edifice she issued forth every morning to seek out the haunts of the literary lions of the past. Milton's house, where he wrote *Paradise Lost,* and Dr. Samuel Johnson's bachelor home in Bolt Court were shrines before which she had formerly in her imagination and now in reality worshipped. She trailed the gentle Charles Lamb through dim yellow halls of the Inner Temple. Charter House held her enthralled for long hours by the thought that Thackeray had played here as a boy, and Queen Elizabeth, as a young woman on the verge of a great career, had slept here one night. In this mood she was attracted less by the present Dickens of Bloomsbury than by the young Dickens who had once lived and written in Furnival's Inn. In the evening after days spent with the past she went home to a lively houseful of young students and barristers, with light conversation, charades, and music to fill the hours until bedtime. No emotion disturbed her stay in London. Her life there was suave, pleasing, and delightful.

Toward the end of her stay Louisa walked out of the house one day, this time not for a ghostly rendezvous, but for an interview with a live publisher. It was something that she had seldom had the courage to do at home. Her *Moods* had not lived up to its promise in America — had in fact been forgotten after the first two months — but her intention was to have it published in England. In one interview she sold it to the English publisher, Routledge, and he asked her to write another novel for him. She walked home on air, a triumphant, happy woman. Dickens, then at the zenith of his career, that day did not feel more successful.

6

When the *Africa* steamed into Boston harbour at eleven o'clock on the night of July 21, 1866, bright moonlight lay over the harbour and city. From the deck Louisa could see the well-known form of Anna Pratt's husband waiting for her on the dock. It was too late to disembark, so she slept on board and left the boat in the fine sunshine the day after. With her brother-in-law she took the train for Concord, where the rest of the family were assembled and waiting. Her arrival was a moving family event.

Louisa's home-coming was the return of a native. In one year she had tried out European life thoroughly and had chosen a life in America. At a time when many American artists and writers believed that Europe was the only home for a talent, Louisa decided to develop hers in her own native environment. She had talked and dreamed for years of living abroad, like the Hawthornes, the Storys, and the Jameses; but she returned home now ready to stay. To be sure, it was only a hypothetical question with her, for she had no means to live abroad; but she settled it as if it were real. She no longer cherished the wish to live abroad.

Miss Weld had done Louisa's career a lasting service. She had obliged her to spend six months in idleness and to live a year without writing. However desperate with boredom Louisa had become at times, there had been no escape from it. When homesickness overcame her, she had to endure the pangs until they ceased. Miss Weld had kept her too busy to do anything except write letters home. " Nine months of hard work and solitary confinement " was the way Mrs. Alcott put it. It was the best thing that could have possibly happened to her. Accustomed to work at tremendous speed and pressure, she had been obliged to lead a sane life all this while; " wasting her time," she called it. Nothing but a great force like Miss Weld could have accomplished it. Louisa, against her will, came home from Europe rested.

But from the moment when she saw her mother weeping in the doorway, the old depression and worry came back. The old demon of tension took possession of her. Family finances began to oppress her. Maybe the sum she had borrowed for her stay in Paris and London seemed a little staggering when she faced the necessity of paying it back, but she had delighted memories to console her. In any case she fell to writing like mad and produced twenty-five stories in her old manner within a year. In less time than that she had worked herself ill. It was another year of silence in her diary.

Beneath this dull laborious life, however, the new Louisa went on existing. Like the green surface of moss beneath an overlay of dead leaves, her new personality lived on. The roots of a new sensitiveness pushed against the smothering force of old moods and passions. Some of the self-confidence she had displayed in London survived beneath the mantle of inferiority she had reassumed as " an Alcott." A core of dignity remained intact through all the drudgery and self-sacrifice of the following year. Louisa was never again the same laborious old maid that Theodore Parker had eulogized.

CHAPTER IX

An American Author

LOUISA MAY ALCOTT, for all the appreciation of her tales, wrote one novel that is lost to history. It was called *Moods*. During the celebration of her centenary, notices about *Moods* appeared stating vaguely that it had once existed; but in the intervening time it had not been mentioned. Written when she was twenty-seven, nothing survives now but a few yellowed volumes testifying to her first ambitious attempt at a novel. It is an almost forgotten book.

Yet *Moods* was after all not her first dash for fame. That was *Hospital Sketches,* made up of letters she had sent home from the Washington hospital. Written later than *Moods* but published first, it had been exceedingly popular. Through it Louisa had experienced her first " dose of fame." An abolitionist book and an abolitionist publisher had given the author only a local celebrity, but that celebrity was, as far as it reached, immense. Boston publishers began to court her, asking for more *Hospital Sketches*. Louisa thought seriously of taking up one of these offers and of going to teach at the Port Royal school for freedmen in order to write her experiences.

Meanwhile came the publication of *Moods*. The manuscript had been hawked about Boston for three years. Bronson Alcott had talked it into several editorial offices, but had forthwith been obliged to call for it again. The last publisher who read it proposed that it should be cut in half. Shuddering at the vandal's suggestion, Louisa sent her father to rescue it. At last the manuscript came to Loring, on a certain auspicious day, and he brought it out. This time Louisa succumbed to what seemed to be inevitable; she consented to cut it by one third. Taking out ten chapters and rewriting the rest, she reduced her two-volume novel to one volume and that a rather brief one. The story was finally published during Christmas week 1864.

Moods, the title, was taken from a passage of Emerson's beginning: " Life is a train of moods like a string of beads . . ." and the passage was placed on her title-page. The heroine of the story, Sylvia Yule, was the beautiful and cherished daughter of a wealthy family. Though only eighteen, she was wooed by a philosophical and gentlemanly lover much older than herself, Geoffrey Moor by name. Into this relationship came a third person, Adam Warwick, a masterful character, who immediately awakened a strong response in Sylvia. Having brought things almost to the point of a proposal, Warwick suddenly and inexplicably vanished. Meantime Geoffrey Moor, unable to win Sylvia's consent to their marriage, had also gone away. Sylvia, pining for Warwick, accidentally encountered knowledge of a former attachment of his, and, in a fit of jealousy, engaged herself to Geoffrey Moor, who had opportunely returned. After they were married, Adam Warwick, having fulfilled some secret vow by his absence, reappeared on the scene and awakened the old fiery response in Sylvia. They confessed their love to each other, while Sylvia decided to keep her love a secret from her husband and to remain a faithful wife. Adam Warwick continued to live in the house as Geoffrey Moor's guest. In an attack of sleep-walking, however, Sylvia betrayed her secret to her husband, who thereupon resolved to go away to Europe and leave her free to make her choice between himself and his friend. Warwick, equally noble, at the last moment accompanied him. Sylvia, left alone with her grief and conflict, fell into a physical decline. Geoffrey Moor, in Europe, received a message from her finally asking him to return. Both he and Warwick interpreted this as meaning that Sylvia had made her choice and Moor in this belief prepared to return. He insisted nevertheless on Warwick's accompanying him, and they set out together on the homeward voyage. Their ship was wrecked within sight of the shore, and Warwick, sacrificing himself to save Moor's life, was drowned. Geoffrey Moor arrived at home only in time for his fading Sylvia to die in his arms.

This dramatic story, modelled in spirit on a romance of Goethe's and written in the style of Hawthorne, with occasional excursions into the style of Dickens, went at first like wildfire. The first edition was exhausted within a week and a second immediately printed. Louisa was very happy. " For a week wherever I went I saw, heard, and talked ' Moods '; found people laughing or crying over it, and was continually told how well it was going, how much it was liked, how fine a thing I'd done. I was glad but not proud, I think, for it has always seemed as if ' Moods ' grew in spite of me, and that I had little to do with it except to put into words the thoughts that would not let me rest until I had." Then quickly and completely the tide turned. Louisa's diary registers the change and mentions the cause. " People seem to think the book finely written, very promising, wise, and interesting; but some fear it isn't moral, because it speaks freely of marriage." The public, engrossed in a lively story, had not at first grasped the immorality of the book until some unknown critic pointed it out. The mere suggestion of immorality was enough to doom a novel in 1865, when all novels were more or less under suspicion. Louisa's was snuffed out in its second edition.

Louisa's reactions can be imagined. She was pained,

bewildered, irate. " I seem to have been playing with edge-tools without knowing it," she complained. " The relations between Warwick, Moor, and Sylvia are pronounced impossible." Not only this, but the dangerous word " affinities " was trotted out and attached to the situation of her characters. The Boston public had already declared its attitude toward the concept in its disapproval of Goethe. This was the main ground of their criticism of her book. In the relations of her characters rather than in a few random unorthodox opinions on the subject of marriage was the immorality of *Moods* alleged to consist. " It was meant to show a life affected by *moods,* not a discussion of marriage," said Louisa ruefully. But the public insisted on viewing it as the latter, with an immoral trend. Louisa decided that their misunderstanding was due to her having shortened the book, and bitterly regretted her compliance.

Yet Louisa had vaguely challenged the rebuff. She had trembled a good deal in reading the proof and had reassured herself by a saying of Emerson's that " what is true for your own private heart is true for others." Her mind had been expressed in a letter to a friend who admired *Hospital Sketches:* " ' Moods ' won't suit you so well, I suspect, for in it I've freed my mind upon a subject that always makes trouble, Love. But being founded upon fact, and the characters drawn from life, it may be of use as all experiences are and serve as a warning at least." This explanation, however, was not one that she could make to the public. Some other proof of the truth of her characters had to be found, for Louisa was too much disturbed by the protest she had aroused to expose the innocent individuals who had sat for her. After that one impulsive and injudicious remark to her friend, she never referred to them. Silence was her only answer to the mild but killing furor.

The originals of her characters are not far to seek, however. Much of the background of her story was taken from the events at Fruitlands, and the emotional situation which developed between Warwick, Sylvia, and Moor was probably suggested by the crisis between Bronson Alcott, Charles Lane, and Abba Alcott. Allowing for the elastic play of Louisa's imagination — she changed the ending in writing it — the facts, atmosphere, and characters are presumably those of Fruitlands.

Louisa Alcott had therefore written about unusual but not impossible people. They were true for her early idealistic time and environment. If she had waited to write *Moods* until after her great divide at Washington, she would never have written it. If the novel had been published as soon as written, it would have had a different reception. *Moods* was a reminiscence of transcendentalism. It belonged to an epoch that had died before the book was published. Its romantic and sentimental atmosphere failed to interest a public disillusioned by wartime. This as much as its alleged immorality made people condemn it.

An interesting item about *Moods* is the light it throws on Louisa Alcott's precocity. The actual events on which it was based had taken place when she was ten and eleven years old. The impression made on her by the emotional situation around her and the ideas then formed about the adults involved in it were so vivid that they remained unforgotten until she was thirty. Parents and educators may draw their own conclusions from this about how much young children who dwell in the midst of grown-up affairs know about their environment. Less brilliant children may perhaps have some portion of Louisa's sensitivity. Her young heart was early attuned to passions beyond her years.

2

After the failure of her first novel Louisa waited nearly four years before writing her second. It seems like a long fallow period for one so ambitious, but to the handicap of discouragement was added the general state of confusion during and after the Civil War. Her absence in Europe was fortunately timed. It was not until 1868 that she sat down again to write another long novel. That year, by a coincidence, was like the year in which she had written *Moods* in being a time of unusual ease and plenty for her family. Louisa had a job as editor of *Merry's Museum*, a magazine for children, at five hundred dollars a year, and her father's lecture tours were doing well. " The year begins well and cheerfully for us all," she wrote in her diary. " For many years we have not been so comfortable." Louisa had the strong Puritan belief in the spur of poverty, but in practice she accomplished more in a state of security.

The story that she produced was *Little Women*. What with all the time that had passed since she wrote *Moods,* what with her resolve to write a very different book from that one, and what with the experiences she had gone through in Europe, her second book was so unlike her first that it scarcely seemed as if the same hand could have written them both. The first novel was more completely lost than ever after *Little Women* had established her fame as an author.

Little Women was due to the focusing of two sets of circumstances. Louisa had had for ten years a plan for writing the story of her own family under the title of " The Pathetic Family." The idea came to her once in Concord while she was listening to her aged grandmother from Wolcott, Connecticut, tell stories. From that time onward the story of " The Pathetic Family " was constantly turning and shaping itself in her mind. The second impetus was given by the request from the publishing house of Roberts Brothers in Boston to write a *girls' story.* That indefatigable literary agent her father came home one day with the message. Louisa did not take kindly to the suggestion at first. " Began at once on the new job; but didn't like it." She allowed another winter's snow to fall on the unwritten story. In May the same publishers, through her father, emphatically repeated the same request. All at once then, perhaps already transformed beneath the winter snows, " The Pathetic Family " reburgeoned in her mind as *Little Women.*

She entered into one of those work-deliriums in which she was accustomed to write her long stories and within six weeks had the first part of *Little Women* completed. In November she began the second part, and this was again a delirious drive lasting about six weeks. The last chapters were written during the Christmas holidays of 1868. The first volume had been published in October and the second appeared in January. The success of the first had been assured before the second was begun. People accepted at last the truth of Louisa's characters.

Little Women was the story of the Alcott family. Angered at the reception of *Moods,* Louisa had resolved: " In my next book . . . the people shall be as ordinary as possible." What she had angrily resolved had been fulfilled pleasantly. She commented, with satisfaction, as she read the proof: " Not a bit sensational, but simple and true, for we really lived most of it." It was the Alcott home presented in its happiest, most vivid light — a transfigured version of their real family life. It was also a war-story, told by one who had been through the war to a generation that remembered it. But it was a cheerful war-story.

The facts in it adhered closely to the actual facts. The title was a phrase which Bronson Alcott often applied to his four daughters. Meg, Jo, Beth, and Amy March were Annie, Lu, Betty, and Abbie May Alcott. Beth and Amy were but slightly disguised forms of the true names of their originals. Meg's name was very probably suggested by Margaret Fuller's. The Marches were the Mays and "*the* Laurences," as Boston was accustomed to call one of its first families, loaned their name to Louisa's elegant Colonel Laurence, as Colonel May loaned him his title. Laurie, or Theodore, was probably called after Louisa's idol, Theodore Parker. Real persons used in the book were Great-aunt Hancock and Aunt Bond, who were cast into one mould to form that noble but disagreeable benefactress Aunt March. Louisa's boarding-house in Boston became one in New York. The place called by the Alcotts *Hillside*, as it was when they lived there, was the home of the March family. And so on; the story was built on a groundwork of numerous real facts. The trail of the "lived" things in *Little Women* was a long one.

The most popular character in the book, after Jo March, was Laurie. Readers besieged the author to know on whom the charming youth was modelled. Louisa finally gave them this answer: "Laurie was a Polish boy, met abroad in 1865." But at another time she wrote to an old pupil of Franklin Sanborn's school: "I put you in my story as one of the best and dearest lads I ever knew. Laurie is you and my Polish boy 'jintly.' " Mr. Alfred Whitman, of Kansas, the old pupil thus addressed, therefore asserted in due time his official claim to be Laurie's original. But in spite of Louisa's letter, it is hard to believe that Whitman had any greater part in Laurie than several other old acquaintances.

Louisa's memory might just as well have lighted on another boy whom she had known in Concord. Fred Willis, who had lived with the family when Louisa was sixteen and shared so many of the experiences used in the book, might also easily have posed for Laurie. Bronson Alcott believed that Willis was the inspiration. " Well, my boy, did you recognize yourself as Laurie in Louisa's book? " he asked Willis cheerfully on meeting him in a Boston railway station. And still farther back in her past was a pair of dark eyes and " a brown boy," William Lane, who belonged to that highly adventurous though tragic world created by her father and Lane. But all these memories, however rich, were incidental. Laurie was really Ladislas Wisniewski.

There is no pursuit more delightful than tracing the sources of Louisa May Alcott's characters. The blind alley in this game has always been the elderly, absentminded personage known as Professor Bhaer. The amiable German professor has always been an exception in the lived background of *Little Women*. He is said to have been the one character in the book that Louisa Alcott made up out of whole cloth. And yet, though never as popular, he is fully as real as all the rest. The public never doubted Professor Bhaer any more than they doubted Meg or Amy; he was a living character in a living book. His creation, according to the accepted critical legend, followed a special and exceptional act on the author's part. Professor Bhaer — odd, human, lovable Professor Bhaer — was no one.

This legend, it may be noted, was not started by Louisa Alcott herself. She never gave any explanation of Professor Bhaer, although she once made a detailed statement about the origin of most of the characters in the book, quite omitting him. It was her friend and biographer, Ednah Dow Cheney, who said: " The demand of the publisher and the public [that Jo marry] was so imperative that she created her German professor, of whom no prototype existed." This was the first appearance of a statement which, coming from a supposedly authoritative source, afterwards became standardized. But in view of Louisa Alcott's complete silence on the subject, one may be permitted to doubt it; especially as she never created any other really important character without having some living prototype in mind.

Professor Bhaer was probably Dr. William Rimmer, a noted man and a famous sculptor. He belonged to a family whose romantic reputation equalled that of the Alcott family. It was a coincidence perhaps that Rimmer's father lived in a humble house just round the corner from the elegant home of Louisa's grandfather. The elder Rimmer was a shoemaker. William Rimmer, the son, started life as an itinerant portrait-painter and developed afterwards into a sculptor and a

DR. WILLIAM RIMMER

teacher of art. In the meantime he had been a practis-
ing physician and was always known as " Dr. Rimmer."
His fame rested on his work as a sculptor, the best-
known example of which is *The Falling Gladiator* in a
Boston museum. In his lifetime, however, he was as
much known for his remarkable personality as for anything else.

Louisa Alcott knew William Rimmer well. He was
her sister May's art-teacher. Rimmer was an inspired
teacher, much as Bronson Alcott was. His career as a
teacher included several years as director of the Cooper
Union School of Design for Women in New York and
a longer period as teacher in the Boston Museum of
Fine Arts. At the time when May Alcott studied with
him, he was holding private classes in Boston. At the
time when *Little Women* was written, he was living in
New York and carrying on his work there in Cooper
Union. After the publicaton of *Little Women* he returned to live in Boston. There are several references
to him in Louisa's journal as May's teacher.

There can be little doubt that Dr. Rimmer was the
original of Professor Bhaer. The professor adheres as
closely to his model as the other characters in the book
adhere to theirs. While some of Professor Bhaer's
traits seem to suggest Bronson Alcott, it is only because
Alcott and Rimmer were similar personalities in some
ways. The gentle, elderly Professor Bhaer at the same
time sounded a more vigorous note than ever was
sounded by Louisa's father. Bronson Alcott is repre-

sented in the book by Mr. March. When the author of *Little Women* brings Mr. March and Professor Bhaer face to face on the same page and allows them to hold a dialogue, it indicates that she had not derived them from one and the same person. There was a literal trend in Louisa Alcott's imagination which would have prevented her from doing that. The same literal tendency caused her to introduce a detail into Professor Bhaer's portrait which betrays his origin. This is the episode about the professor's wearing the paper hat and forgetting to remove it. It is the well-known episode in the life of Louis XVI. Having carefully created her German professor of the exiled type familiar in the '50's, and having endowed him with the virtues of democracy, gallantry, and patience, Louisa added this further detail from the life of an autocratic French king. It slipped into the record because Dr. Rimmer, American citizen though he was, traced his ancestry through a dramatic family tradition back to a branch of the royal house of France. It was one of the most noteworthy facts about him. Professor Bhaer, with his strong German accent, fell into an alien French role. Homer nodded.

A question arises concerning Mrs. Cheney's statement: if a fiction, was it made innocently or intentionally? Mrs. Cheney personally comes into the story because she was one of the adoring feminine cult which gathered in Dr. Rimmer's studio. Mrs. Cheney as well as May Alcott was his pupil in art. She could scarcely have failed to recognize his likeness to Professor Bhaer. Her explanation must therefore have been purposely made to shield someone from embarrassing inferences. Boston was a small world in those days. The incidental result was that she wiped out one of the most picturesque and living elements in the background of *Little Women*. It is in the true relation between that book and its sources that much of its charm for the world consists. That Dr. Rimmer was one of these sources there can be little doubt.

" We lived it," said Louisa of the book. Professor Bhaer was a true story with all the rest.

3

A book that was written in twelve weeks has lived sixty years and is still living. Its continuing vitality is seen in the throngs who witnessed the cinema revival of the story. The copyright, extended to the longest possible legal limit, eventually expired. But the public has noticed no difference. It has always demanded its yearly quantity of *Little Women*, unaware of whether there was a copyright or not on this book which it has always regarded as its own.

Neither Louisa nor the publishers foresaw this success. Louisa, perhaps only a little more than the publishers, believed in the story. But she took her cue from them and awaited its appearance without excitement. Roberts Brothers allowed the first volume, all completed and ready for print as it was, to lie untouched for several months. They were soon to regret every week that they had lost.

Its success was instantaneous. Boston capitulated at once; the city was wildly excited about it. " Merchants and lawyers meeting on their way down-town in the morning," says Mr. Stearns, " said to each other, ' Have you read *Little Women*? ' It was the rage in '69, as Pinafore was in '78." The year which saw the publication of *Little Women* was the year in which the first transcontinental railroad was completed. Copies of *Little Women* travelled swiftly across the country on the first transcontinental trains. They sped to the far ends of the re-united States. The book was read impartially in the North, the South, and the West. At one bound Louisa Alcott had outstripped every other Concord writer of her time. The fame of Emerson and Thoreau was pale by comparison. As for Bronson Alcott's *Tablets,* just previously published, there is no word to describe the difference. One of the greatest tributes to the selflessness of Alcott's character is the cordial delight he took in Louisa's success.

The Life of a Book is what one might call the history of *Little Women*. Most books are born to perish, but *Little Women* was born to survive. Ten, twenty-five, fifty years later, it could still be discovered in the same outstanding place. Thousands of girls' books have been written since, but none could dislodge it. It became a perennial best-seller, the copies sold in this country alone amounting to millions before it became impossible to keep any account of them. Its exceeding popularity in England is little realized in this country — as little as the prominent part it plays in the literature of foreign countries. It has grown to be one of the world's classics. With the twentieth century it began to sell better than it had in the nineteenth. Perhaps it is as well known the world over as any of Shakespeare's plays.

A book which has touched and continues to touch so many human hearts must be a great work. There has always been some reluctance among literary critics to admit the worth of *Little Women*. They have found it too simple, too sweet. These are the faults not so much of the book as of the age in which it was written. Underneath is a truth almost severe.

"In an age when there prevailed a prim ritual of manners," says Miss Lucile Gulliver, "and an exaggerated reticence in the matter of all private affairs, Louisa Alcott suddenly spoke out. . . . There is no doubt that it is this courageous candor which has made Miss Alcott's greatness." As usual with sudden and revolutionary performances, there was for Louisa Alcott's act a slow preparation. Long, long before *Little Women* Emerson noted this in his journal: " Alcott . . . in his native town . . . went about and invited all the people, his relatives and friends, to meet him at five o'clock in the school-house, on Sunday evening. Thither they came, and he sat at the desk and gave them the story of his life. Some went away discontented be-

cause they had not heard a sermon, as they hoped."
Alcott was ever a voice crying in the wilderness and pre-
paring the way for another. Louisa Alcott also told the
story of her life; and the spirit which made her bold
enough to tell it was the spirit of her father. Looking
back through the years, she saw them with objectivity
and honesty, and with the courage she had learned from
her father, and so she portrayed them.

Knowing the sources of her story makes it possible to
see how her mind, playing over the material, introduced here and there the changes of genius. Slight as
they were, they gave the book its lift into the empyrean.
How masterly to change the exotic background of William Rimmer into the familiar background of a German exile in America! The German exiles had fought
in the Civil War. This gave the touch of reality that
was better than the truth. What grace divine told
Louisa that Vevey was only another Concord after all
and the Lake of Geneva only another Concord River?
What implacable sense of proportion told her that it
was much more suitable to marry May to the elegant
Laurie, and Jo to an intellectual rough-hewn professor,
although in real life the attraction was just vice versa?
At the same mysterious command she changed the ages
of the sisters, so that they were brought closer together,
and put back their adolescent years into the period of
the Civil War. In such slight but important creations
the power of the artist shows itself. Some emotion

deeper than artistic creation caused her to make the character of Marmee one of unbroken perfection and sweetness. This was a dream so fundamental in her life that she probably never once aroused from it, waking or sleeping.

Little Women is a story about love: a novel. For only a novel could achieve such abounding and enduring popularity. The story of Jo and Laurie is a gay and charming romance, with a touch of autumnal sadness in the ending which allies it with love-stories like Romeo and Juliet's. In no part of the book does the story attain a more convincing reality. The episode is one of the permanent romances of literature. Those who have overlooked it have done so because they were blinded by a preconceived and erroneous idea of Louisa Alcott as a person. Only in blindness could Gamaliel Bradford say of her: " There is no indication that, in her own case, there was any disappointed love "; or Katharine Fullerton Gerould decide: " Miss Alcott writes as one who had never loved "; and Frank Sanborn declare: " She was incapable of a successful novel." Though Louisa often expressed herself as adverse to marriage, the philosophy out of which she wrote her stories did not sustain that opinion. All of her heroines were married. The " Little Women " were all happily married at the end, including the ambitious Jo. The romantic tenor of the book has formed a large part of its appeal; but because it was written by Louisa Alcott and was intended for girls, no one was willing to admit that it was a novel. All the while it has been one of the world's most thrilling love-stories.

In this tale Louisa wrote a book for everybody. A story about adolescents, it had a happy reach above and below the magic border-line of fleeting youth. At a modern theatre production of *Little Women,* a critic looked over the audience and said: " ' Little Women ' can no longer be classed as juvenile." It was never a book for juvenile readers alone. On its first appearance it was read with joy by men and women as well as by girls and boys. If it has been less read by adults since, it is because they have all had the opportunity to read it earlier. The appearance of the story in a new form on the screen called forth anew the old response from all ages. No book has ever had a more democratic appeal.

What draws this diverse public is the love-story and the presentation of the home. People have read *Little Women* avidly not only for its high-keyed romance but also for its gentler and quieter drama of the home. *Little Women* is the romance *par excellence* of family affection. Nothing so simple had ever before or has since been attempted, and this simplicity is one of the things that has made the book a classic.

Also it was the first purely American novel. There had been previously colonial novels, Puritan novels, Indian novels, Southern novels, and New England novels; but no American novel had appeared up to then. *Little Women* was the first novel written that reflected the Union. Considering the sore time in which it was written, the author's abolitionist background, and her earlier writings, its unbiased attitude toward the war bears noticing. While the social background of the book is pure New England, the home pictured could be any home in the North or South during the war. Since writing *Hospital Sketches* Louisa had gained a wider view of the world. Europe and Ladislas Wisniewski had done this for her. None of the bitterness of the late civil strife invaded the atmosphere of *Little Women*. It was a war-story which both sides could read. It flowed through the nation, passing all barriers and acting as one of the great healers of the time. The South, which had hated and anathematized Harriet Beecher Stowe, embraced the abolitionist Louisa May Alcott with unreserved warmth and affection. Southern girls were brought up on *Little Women* as generally as were other girls. They had no thought of the author as other than one of themselves. Louisa May Alcott was everywhere regarded as an American author and *Little Women* as an American book.

4

It was one of the faults of Louisa's rather too rigid character that she could never acknowledge an indebtedness; except to her mother, to whom she said she owed all, she never expressed any obligation. She insisted proudly that she had climbed the up-hill road alone with " never a literary friend to lend a helping hand." This was somewhat exaggerated. The literary Brahmins of Boston had naturally paid no attention to the upstart daughter of a threadbare Bronson Alcott. But others had come to her aid. There was first of all Emerson, who had inspired her first novel. There was also Frank Sanborn, who had brought out her first publications and had urged her to write more, assuring her that " any publisher this side of Baltimore would be glad to get a book." Moncure D. Conway, another abolitionist friend, has also guided and advised her in her early struggles. Furthermore that never-tiring handy-man her father had from the first peddled her wares and brought her fertile suggestions. Of no little importance had been the attention of the two Henry Jameses, father and son, who had both helped to make Louisa see herself as an author of assured promise.

When Louisa published *Moods,* Henry James the younger was barely twenty-one. With a precocity like Louisa's, he had already begun his literary career by writing book-reviews. A year of university study had been followed by a year of bad health, and academic training sat lightly upon him. He had in the main the same preparation as she — a background of idealism, literary home-life, intellectual preoccupations, and intense family affection. Except for the difference made by more extensive travel and schooling, young Henry James was a family product on the order of Louisa.

At twenty-one he was writing for several literary journals. A reviewer of novels chiefly, he was a highly respected, though anonymous (all book-reviews were unsigned in those days) critic of fiction. The works of authors like Trollope, George Eliot, Alexandre Dumas, Victor Hugo were assigned to him for judgment. Long literary essays purporting to come from a man twice his years dropped from his pen and revealed him as no tyro even at that early age. It was in the course of this work that one of the first copies of *Moods* that left the press fell into his hands. The whole family read it and the elder James made capital of it for one of his jokes. Meeting Alcott on the street, he said: " We have all been reading Louisa's *Dumps*! "

To young Henry James, with his impressionable spirit and his eager state of mind, *Moods* came as more than a book; it came as an experience. He realized, if no one else did, that the rather lanky and hard-working daughter of Bronson Alcott, who lived in the house next door to Hawthorne, had caught the authentic fire. Hawthorne was for young Henry the great god of Concord. All the other Concordians were philosophers, or naturalists, or poets. Hawthorne alone represented for him the supreme god: the novelist. Rather he had represented that, for now the great Hawthorne was dead, one of the civilian casualties of the war. He had died without leaving any visible successor. Whoever might write the next *Scarlet Letter* was not even shadowily discernible on the horizon. Whence and how the new creative spirit might arise occupied the critic of fiction. He had not himself written a novel. Louisa May Alcott, ten years older and to this extent at least better prepared to inherit Hawthorne's mantle, startled him into excited attention with her first novel. That this vivid story came out of Concord and that its author was the next-door neighbour of Hawthorne was enough to excite the sensitive young James.

He wrote one of his long book-reviews for a New York journal. In it he defended the morals of *Moods,* the aspect of the book which had aroused so much criticism in Boston. Remarking that " Miss Alcott had written her version of the old story of the husband, the wife, and the lover," and adding nonchalantly that " the French do that sort of thing better," he offered it as his opinion that the book was innocent of immoral teaching or of any teaching whatsoever. " We have seen it asserted that her book claims to deal with the ' doctrine of affinities ' . . . but we are inclined to think that our author has been somewhat maligned. Her book is, to our perception, innocent of any doctrine whatever." After this tribute to the integrity of the story-teller in Louisa, he went on to arraign her for her " ignorance of human nature." He sought to prove his point by analysing the character of her romantically drawn hero, venting his indignation on his unnatural personality. " Women appear to delight in the conception of men who shall be insupportable to men." He considered the husband in the story to be a tolerable character, but weak; and the heroine to be amiable and engaging, but too young. In spite of these minor faults, he conceded the book great cleverness and imagination. " Imagination does not seem to us too grand a word. If Miss Alcott's experience of human nature has been small, as we should suppose, her admiration of it is nevertheless great. Putting aside Adam's treatment of Ottila, she sympathizes with none but great things. . . . With the exception of two or three celebrated names, we know not, indeed, to whom, in this country, unless to Miss Alcott, we are to look for a novel above the average." Surely this might be called encouragement, from a potential rival.

Continuing, he gave Louisa this plain-spoken advice: " There is no reason why Miss Alcott should not write a very good novel, provided she will be satisfied to describe that which she has seen. Miss Alcott doubtless knows men and women well enough to deal successfully with their every-day virtues and temptations, but not well enough to handle great dramatic passions. When such a novel comes, as we doubt not it eventually will, we shall be the first to welcome it." It did come. Could the advice of Henry James have had something to do with shaping it into a simple story of every-day virtues and temptations? Perhaps this advice, acting on Louisa's sensitive spirit along with the more profound experiences which followed after *Moods,* made her more willing to write a simple tale.

If Henry's advice made an impression on Louisa, her

personality made an impression on him. They dined together at the elder James's dinner-table soon after the publication of *Moods*. Henry was unusually loquacious in the presence of his father. " Being a literary youth," said Louisa, with one of her occasional sarcasms, " he gave me advice as if he had been eighty and I a girl." Henry could not be in the presence of so much talent without being stimulated by it, and this was talent which had written a novel. He observed their silent and reserved guest that night with intentness.

There was little or no personal relation between them after this. Henry James went abroad soon after Louisa had returned from Europe, and stayed there, while Louisa remained in Concord. The young critic began to write novels; several were published, with no outstanding success. He then wrote *Daisy Miller* and his name went through America. The skeleton of this story should be familiar to us. The scene is laid in Vevey; the heroine is an unchaperoned American girl. The heroine falls in love with the hero during a boat-ride on the lake. Chaperonage, by the way, is taken as a serious question in this story. The hero and heroine meet a second time in Rome but after this they part forever. This is all exceedingly reminiscent of Louisa's adventures with her Polish youth in Vevey and Paris; they were to have met in Rome, but never did. Louisa Alcott had already used the Vevey episode for her Americanized Jo and Laurie, and Henry James used it all over again in his first successful novel of manners. Not often is a romance found to be so fruitful.

Louisa Alcott disliked *Daisy Miller* very much. In one of her short stories she took occasion to warn American girls against the type represented by James's heroine. As Louisa seldom mentioned the works of her contemporaries in her diaries, this reference to a story of the day in a piece of fiction is rather surprising. She was evidently more than usually impressed by *Daisy Miller,* and the feeling aroused was not altogether pleasant.

When Henry James was twenty-one and Louisa Alcott was the newly fledged author of *Moods,* he wrote this note about the heroine: " We regret to say that Miss Alcott takes her up in her childhood. We are utterly weary of stories about precocious little girls." This is an odd objection on the part of a young man who was in the future to write as many stories about precocious little girls as Henry James. Mr. Pierre La Rose has pointed out the discrepancy between this and Henry James's later stories, *The Turn of the Screw* and *What Maisie Knew*. One might add with equal appropriateness *Daisy Miller* and *The Awkward Age*. Few novelists have betrayed the same partiality for juvenile heroines as Henry James, and his juvenile heroines are all deadly precocious.

A further discrepancy can be seen between Henry James's dislike for Louisa's middle-aged hero in *Moods* and his own later heroes. At twenty-one he warmly condemned Louisa's Warwick as a creature " who has travelled all over the world, lives on a mysterious patrimony, and spends his time in breaking the hearts and wills of demure little school-girls who answer him with ' Yes, sir ' and ' No, sir.' " When one thinks of Winterbourne, Sir Claude, and Vanderbank, one wonders why Henry James was not more charitable toward Louisa's Warwick. If he really disliked the type, he must have been hypnotized by her example. His own partiality for his transcendental heroes convicts him otherwise of great inconsistency.

Henry James and Louisa Alcott had this in common: they had both grown up in an atmosphere of unfulfilled literary ambition and had come to realize, as children do in such a household, that literature must be made to succeed or it must be given up. To this extent they were both practical. They stood close together at the beginning of their careers, and the mutual influence was perhaps stronger than anyone realizes.

5

Louisa had always sold the copyrights of her books outright for two or three hundred dollars. When she came to Thomas Niles with the manuscript of *Little Women,* he offered as usual to buy it outright, but suggested as an alternative that she keep the copyright for herself. It would be interesting to know what sum she was offered for the book outright; we may assume that it was nothing unusual, for the publishers were not especially excited by the manuscript before it was published. The prosperity of the Alcott family in the year 1868 enabled her to keep the copyright. Usually a few hundred dollars in the hand meant more to her than twice that much in the bush, but as things were going rather well at home just then, Louisa felt she could afford to take an unprecedented step.

Thomas Niles was the mainspring of Roberts Brothers. He was an acquaintance of Louisa Alcott's father and was publishing a book by Alcott called *Tablets* when he sent the message home to Louisa about writing a book for girls. His attitude about the copyright was only an attitude of fair dealing, but to Louisa it seemed like the greatest philanthropy. She had not been fortunate in her experience with publishers. Samuel Goodrich, the famous " Peter Parley," had sweated her as he had sweated Nathaniel Hawthorne; Redpath had made a good thing out of *Hospital Sketches* without her getting any the richer; and Loring had deserted *Moods* at the first gun fired from Beacon Hill. Meeting the honourable and dignified attitude of Roberts Brothers, she responded with almost unnecessary gratitude.

Louisa's first step under the resulting prosperity was to pay all family bills. Doctors' bills dating back for ten years, the balance still owing for her trip abroad, loans from Mrs. Alcott's relatives — all family obligations were promptly wiped out. It was an unprecedented state of things in the Alcott family history. For a while

Louisa enjoyed a sensation of plenty. Her second step was to make some investments. "Gave Samuel E. Sewall $200 to invest." And still the wealth came rolling in. "Made up $1,000 for Samuel E. Sewall to invest. Now I have $1200 for a rainy day and no debts." Here was indeed a new experience for Louisa Alcott.

Her prosperity apparently survived the panic of 1869 unimpaired. Either Cousin Samuel E. Sewall had invested very wisely or *Little Women* repaired every loss. While the rest of the world was struggling in the panic, she continued still to be better off than ever before in her life. In the winter of 1868–9, she moved into Boston and tried life in a new, upholstered, palm-decorated hotel. It was Louisa's first introduction to steam heat and an elevator. Perhaps steam heating was less well developed than it is now, but she found the banging and exploding of the pipes insufferable. The sound of the wind whistling around the top-floor apartment to which the elevator had whisked her was too irksome to be borne. It was not the kind of sky-parlour that she was used to. She soon left the elegant hotel quarters for a brick-front lodging-house in Chauncey Street. But in that uncomfortable and uncongenial environment she wrote and completed the second part of *Little Women*.

May Alcott had begun to play an important part in Louisa's life. When Louisa came back from her year abroad, she found that her younger sister had grown up and was now another woman like herself. It was at

May's suggestion that Louisa went to live at the Hotel Bellevue, taking May with her. " She doesn't enjoy quiet corners as I do," said Louisa, " so we . . . had a queer time . . . eating in a marble café, and sleeping on a sofa-bed, that we might be genteel." The two spent the following August at a fashionable summer hotel on Mt. Desert — an experiment which pleased Louisa better. She could always enjoy the seashore and grow gay and young in the salt atmosphere.

Louisa's only personal extravagance was doctors. About this time she began to go to expensive specialists, starting a round that was to continue for years. After finishing *Little Women* in a " vortex," she was, as might be expected, used up. But it never occurred to her to heal herself by taking a vacation. She had scarcely undoubled her limbs from writing these four hundred pages when she accepted a request to write four short stories immediately. Though finances were better, she did not dare to refuse the offer of twenty dollars apiece. Rheumatism and neuralgia racked her frame, and still further suffering came from a peculiar complaint in her throat. She lost her voice. But the rheumatism was confined to her left arm, and the loss of her voice only prevented her from acting, not from writing. With her left arm in a sling and her throat bound up, she turned out pages and pages of new manuscript. When pain overwhelmed her, she repaired to doctors and specialists instead of resting. She was treated by nine or ten of the leading physicians of Boston within two years. " No rest for the brains that earn the money," was her comment. She had the firm belief of her time that brains were dangerous to the body and that medical treatment had to be called in to relieve this danger.

Suffering and ill as she was, Louisa did not feel old. Her aches and pains were associated with a strong zest for life and with youthful spirits which brought her nearer to her sister in age. Besides, May Alcott, what with the slow passage of the Civil War and her prolonged application to the study of art, had grown to be about thirty herself. Her influence continued to develop and take hold in Louisa's life.

The winter of 1869–70 was spent by the two in the sedate environs of Pinckney Street. It was a period of more social contact than Louisa had ever experienced. Her acquaintances were of the new feminine type. The independent woman she now met in Boston was the rising phenomenon of the age. She had made great strides since Louisa's earlier discovery of her in church and charity work. Through May Alcott, who belonged to the newer type by age and temperament, Louisa was introduced to it. She lived May's life and, in spite of her ailments and specialists, enjoyed the adventure. It was a winter of friendships and good times, one of the few periods of the kind in Louisa Alcott's life.

In the cold and snows of Pinckney Street, Louisa wrote *An Old-Fashioned Girl*. It was the first book she wrote under the stress and strain of great success, but the story showed no ill effects from that or from her bad health. It repeated the charm of *Little Women* and contained the best of Louisa herself — her ease, her honesty, her ineffable sparkle. It pleased the audience of girls in some ways even better than its predecessor, because it reflected so vividly the life around them. The delight with which it was received would be difficult to describe. No other American author had ever been hailed and read with so much excitement.

Louisa fled from it all in a trip to Europe. To go abroad under her own financial power was a reckless extravagance, but the continued yield of *Little Women* seemed sufficient to justify her rashness. Her family were comfortable, her investments had risen, and still the pleasant dollars came flowing in. Still she would scarcely have gone but for a rare piece of good luck. One of her Boston friends, Miss Alice Bartlett, invited May to go to Europe as her guest, with the proviso that Louisa should also accompany them. This opportune offer enabled her to flee at the right time.

She parted with her father and mother more in May's manner than in her own. The parental Alcotts were sent off to Concord the day before, and she went to the South Station escorted by a gay party of friends. This time she was leaving for Europe by way of New York.

The picture continues with two tall ladies seated on the train speeding swiftly on the first lap of their journey. It was the first day of April 1870. " Fit day for *my* undertaking, I thought," noted Louisa ruefully in her diary. Spinsters both, obviously, despite May's golden hair and stylish air, the travellers radiated decorum; but they also radiated purpose and ambition. Louisa was dressed very plainly; she had made almost no preparations for the trip, working on *An Old-Fashioned Girl* almost up to the moment of taking the train. While her fellow-travellers bought and read the first freshly printed copies, she sat demurely in her place and rejected the copy the newsboy offered her. That the travellers were ladies was apparent, for a male relative, their brother-in-law, had come along to help them with their tickets and baggage.

The next morning the same ladies, both very tall, the one light, the other dark, accompanied by a third spinster lady, might have been seen boarding a French liner, the *Lafayette,* headed for Brest; and, standing by the rail in a high gale, they waved good-bye to the man standing on the dock.

This second trip of Louisa's to Europe lasted again for a year. It began gaily as the first holiday she had ever allowed herself in her life. She saw herself as enjoying a well-earned vacation and having legitimate pleasure in a friend's congenial society. What she would formerly have regarded as self-indulgence seemed her right. It was the period of her life which came nearest to being free from care and responsibility. She shared in May's delight. It was a turning-point in May's career. She had come to the end of her long apprenticeship in Boston and was now studying art in London, Rome, and Paris. It was the fulfilment of a long-cherished dream of Louisa's. She had launched her sister on her career and she was herself safe and secure in her own. They were both happy, independent women.

CHAPTER X

The Promised Land

THE MOST triumphant part of Louisa's second trip to Europe was that she paid her own travelling expenses. It was still a remarkable thing for a woman to make the grand tour on her own earnings. Louisa might have paid her sister May's expenses also at this time, but she did not trust her new-found prosperity enough. The saying that " the Alcotts can't make money," however much she disproved it, stuck in her crop and made her distrustful of the evidence. And who could say at that date that the yearly yield from *Little Women* would be more regular than a farmer's crop?

She set off for Europe then under favourable financial conditions. With " Pa and Ma " nicely established for the year with her sister Annie, and their board-bill paid in advance, she could dismiss the elderly charges from her mind. Though she was rather invalided, she was well prepared for illness. " A scarlet army blanket, with U.S. in big black letters on it, enveloped her travelling medicine-chest." A doctor whom she met on her travels prescribed a new drug for her rheumatism, which she hopefully added to her collection and dosed herself with according to his advice. Whether from the drug or from rest and diversion she *did* get better; she had not for a long time been so cheerful or so young as when she started through Europe in the spring of 1870.

Louisa's party meandered through France along an unbeaten track. Alice Bartlett, their cicerone, was an experienced tourist. She led them through out-of-the-way villages, past gorse-clad fields, country fairs, and ruined castles, and established them in quaint pensions where they were charged little and entertained deliciously. " Plummy — " said Louisa, " plummy and lovely." They spent six heavenly weeks thus in Dinan, strolling about the market-place, taking drives in donkey-carts, and visiting the ancient châteaux and druid monuments. Thence they wandered through Tours, Blois, Orléans, Bourges, and Lyons, noting history as they went. " What a set of rascals those old kings and queens were! " commented Louisa. They finally dropped anchor in Geneva. At the Hotel Metropole, they donned their best gowns and promenaded elegantly on the terrace above the azure lake. This was all for Louisa Alcott such a holiday as she had never known.

Travelling with a cheerful friend was an initiation

in the lighter side of touring for her. Miss Bartlett was
a poet, though unknown to fame, and they vied in
humorous verses along the way. There were many innocent elegances in Miss Bartlett's life which were new
to Louisa. Manicurists and hairdressers derived their
profit from Miss Bartlett's example. One thing that
amazed her was that Alice " never seemed to have any
clothes, yet was always well and appropriately dressed."
To Louisa clothes of any kind had always been a struggle. She caught the idea from her companion that with
means one could dress well without paying so much
attention to it. Having means now, she tried it. Miss
Bartlett's catholicity toward food was another surprise.
The daughter of the vegetarian Alcott had departed
sufficiently from her upbringing to down plain beef
and mutton, but eels, blood puddings, and kidneys revolted her. No amount of humorous poetizing on Miss
Bartlett's part could help her over this hurdle. There
she stuck, serious and incorrigible, at the barrier.

A lucky chance landed her one night in a hotel bedroom facing the back-stage of an opera. Robed in her
night-gown and a bed-quilt, she witnessed the back-
stage performance even to watching the man aloft in
the wings make the thunder and lightning. It brought
back the thrill of the days when she and her sister Anna
had played Roderigo and Zara, drawing the curtains,
setting up the tower, and shifting the scenery. Neither
Miss Bartlett nor May could share the rapture of that
night, and ardently did Louisa long to have her sister

Anna with her — Anna who was so safely sheltered now in a home with husband and babies.

Except for some rough winds in Brittany, nature had smiled upon them during the trip, nature but not man. While they had been peacefully skirting the south of France, the Franco-Prussian War had been inundating the north. They had kept too far from Paris to hear the rumours of war and not until they reached Switzerland did they realize what was happening. Louisa resisted the whole truth at first. " The breaking out of this silly little war between France and Prussia will play the deuce with our letters," she wrote the home-people. But as the war thundered louder, Louisa's apprehension increased. It looked as if the way to Italy might again be blocked. The war threatened to be a great personal calamity; she might be stuck in Switzerland for the winter. Furthermore it looked almost certain that she could not now return to Paris as she had planned while devoting the whole bright summer to rural France. In Paris had centred the brightest dream of Louisa's life — a dream which had faded to dimness meanwhile, but which had never entirely lost a faint glow. Now at the thunderous march of Bismarck's troops it dimmed suddenly to ashes. She would not see Paris again, not come again into that sparkling presence in which she had once tasted pure happiness. Foolish Louisa, not to know that dead dreams are better buried thus and covered over forever by living fiction!

With her two companions she pushed on to Vevey

and dropped her bags at the Pension Paradis. There they waited for six weeks, hoping for some favourable turn in the Franco-Prussian War. A decisive turn came, but it only availed to cut off Paris the more effectually from American tourists. They might return to England by way of Germany; or they might go on to Italy. But Paris was in the hands of Bismarck. Some refugee families from France appeared at the Pension Paradis. "Ten families applied here yesterday." But no Polish names were among them.

Louisa spent the time studying French, rather against her will, with her sister May. She moped and fretted against their bad luck and spent many hours idly watching the boys at play at the school next door. Alice Bartlett urged her to abandon her vacation and write. But she could not write. After months of gaiety and high spirits she suddenly felt tired, listless, and sad.

In this mood she had a vivid dream which she related in detail to her sister Anna. " I was returning to Concord after my trip, and was alone. As I walked from the station I missed Mr. Moore's house, and turning the corner, found the scene so changed that I did not know where I was. Our house was gone, and in its place stood a . . . castle, with towers and arches and lawns and bridges. . . . Somehow I got into it without meeting any of you, and wandered about trying to find my family. At last I came across Mr. Moore, papering a room, and asked him where his house was. He didn't know me, and said, ' Oh! I sold it to Mr. Alcott for his school, and we live in Acton now.' ' Where did Mr. Alcott get the means to build this great concern? ' I asked. ' Well, he *gave* his own land, and took the great pasture his daughter left him, — the one that died some ten years ago.' ' So I am dead, then,' says I to myself, feeling so queerly. ' Government helped build this place, and Mr. Alcott has a fine college here,' said Mr. Moore, papering away again.

" I went on, wondering at the news, and looked into a glass to see how I looked dead. I found myself a fat old lady, with grey hair and specs, — very like Elizabeth P. Peabody. I laughed, and coming to a Gothic window, looked out and saw hundreds of young men and boys . . . roaming about the parks and lawns, and among them was Pa, looking as he looked thirty years ago, with brown hair and a big white neckcloth. . . . He looked so plump and placid and young and happy I was charmed to see him, and nodded; but he didn't know me; and I was so grieved and troubled at being a Rip Van Winkle, I cried, and said I had better go away and not disturb anyone, — and in the midst of my woe, I woke up."

" I can see how the dream came," she continued, " for I have been looking at Silling's boys in their fine garden, and wishing I could go in and know the dear little lads walking about there, in the forenoon. I had got a top-knot at the barber's, and talked about my grey hairs, and looking in the glass thought how fat and old I was getting; and had shown . . . Pa's picture."

After this dream Louisa felt much better. In her vision she had lived through the pain and bitterness of a reunion with one she loved, one who was immortally young and happy, and he had not known her because she was so old and fat and grey. The worst that could happen to her had happened to her in her dream, and in her vision she had lived through it with tears.

After having this dream and writing it to her sister, Louisa set forth with her companions for Italy. A glorious adventure was crossing the Alps by *diligence,* realizing a thrill long deferred. " It was very exciting, — the general gathering of sleepy travellers in the dark square . . . the slow winding up, up, up out of the valley toward the sun, which came slowly over the great hills, rising as we never saw it rise before. The still, damp pine-forests kept us in shadow a long time after the white mountain-tops began to shine. Little by little we wound through a great gorge, and then the sun came dazzling between these grand hills, showing us a new world. Peak after peak of the Bernese Oberland rose behind us, and great white glaciers lay before us. . . . Here and there were refuges, a hospice, and a few *chalets,* where shepherds live their wild, lonely lives. In the P.M. we drove rapidly down toward Italy through the great Valley of Gondo, — a deep rift in rock . . . and just wide enough for the road and a wild stream that was our guide . . . a fit gateway to Italy, which soon lay smiling before us." This was in October and attended by the most balmy weather. They lingered among the Italian lakes and took their leisurely way through a necklace of cities to Rome. In the Piazza Barberini they hired a flat for the winter and became householders.

To her great surprise, Louisa found herself with a ready-made social circle. Miss Bartlett was one of those wealthy early American tourists for whom a semi-residence in Rome was a necessary part of their culture. She introduced her friends to English-American society. Louisa, who had expected to be overwhelmed by the antiquity and sublimity of Rome, was much disillusioned by this group of her contemporaries. " The order of performance was gossip, tea, music; then music, tea, and gossip." Her disillusionment extended to the marble antiques in the Capitol: the ladies with their hair done *à la sponge* had no glamour and the statues of Nero and the rest were statues of brutes and bad men. Pleasant society in Rome had taken away its grandeur. Her one great joy was that May was having art lessons in the eternal city. To see Michelangelo gave her for the first time faith in her sister's career.

The winter was cold. The rain fell in torrents, and icicles hung from the eaves and cornices. Louisa hugged her warm, comfortable apartment, a blessing that she owed to the lively Miss Bartlett, and wore heavy furs when she went out. She had seen Rome now and she began to think in a leisurely way about going home again. The objects of her trip had been accomplished or else had decisively failed of accomplishment, and she was in a mood to return to prosaic life again. A few more months without strain or responsibility, which she had every reason to expect at this time, might have effectually restored her health.

But circumstances conspired against her. To her, there in Rome, sequestered as it seemed from any but petty misfortunes, the direst shock and sorrow came speeding. The little group at home, about whom she felt so safe, had been violently struck by fate. John Pratt, her brother-in-law, had died suddenly. The news reached her just before Christmas. The last member of the family she had seen on leaving, the one on whom all the others depended in her absence, the protecting genius of her sister and her sister's little boys, quiet John Pratt had without warning ceased to exist.

For Louisa it was impossible to endure sorrow and shock with patience and waiting. Her temperament impelled her to a more positive reaction. She decided that she must do something at once to help Anna and her boys, and with this thought to prod her, she began to write furiously. *Little Men* was written in the Roman apartment in three weeks and was sent off, when completed, by mail to Boston.

Little Men, though as a whole not equal to *Little Women,* contained one of Louisa's finest bits of writing in the description of the death of John Pratt. The dream she had written to Anna and the educational theories of the young father of her dream supplied her with the background of the story. The tale was touched with the sadness of her family's recent loss, as it seemed that only in her dream-world could Louisa learn to survive these ruptures. *Little Men* resumed the saga of the March family as it was laid down at the end of *Little Women*. Though she often said she did not like sequels, she was past mistress of the art of carrying on from one story to the next. The death of John Brooke, like the love-story of Jo and Laurie, illustrates how perfectly Louisa could translate into literature the most intimate experiences of her life.

Though six months remained of the trip, there was little left that was eventful in it. The tour really came to an end in Rome. A hurried return through Germany landed the travellers in London. Louisa had a glimpse of old London acquaintances, one more encounter with fine clothes and manners, another pilgrimage to the haunts of Dickens, and she was ready to sail for home again.

As she had already decided in Rome, she left May behind to continue her art studies. May had finished her year as Miss Bartlett's companion; and now Louisa, awakening to the reality of her sister's ambition, boldly undertook to support her abroad. Though she could not reconcile May's many flirtations with true ambition, Europe had brought her to the point of taking a blind chance. Culture, for which she professed to have so great a resistance, had influenced her.

2

One notes in the returned traveller the first signs of regarding herself as old. She was on the verge of forty. Louisa had habitually thought of herself as a boy until she was twenty-five. At twenty-five she had decided to think of herself as a spinster. At this third stage of her life she just as decidedly began to think of herself as an old lady. The *parti pris* represented the change in her feelings about the past. She had seen Europe without the Pole, and somehow in the confusion of the Franco-Prussian War letters had ceased to come from him.

Affairs at home were anything but cheerful. Her mother and Anna under one roof were a trial. Her mother had aged greatly within the year. Abba's emotions had come to centre more and more around her youngest, and the departure of this daughter of thirty to a remote world had been a severe wrench. She had had to endure the family tragedy of the winter without either May or Louisa. Abba was ill. Louisa saw this at a glance on her return. One of the things that made her feel old was her mother's obviously failing condition.

The little household at Orchard House all rushed with one accord into Louisa's arms. It was both touching and exasperating to see how helplessly and confidingly they all leaned on the only one who was successful. She paid the bills, nursed the sick, and either washed the dishes or managed the servant who did it.

She became again a victim of sleeplessness, and for the
first time it reached such a crisis that she resorted to
morphine. It seems odd that with her devotion to fresh
air and exercise and outdoor life she should not have
turned to this form of relief. But she was still under
the influence of the belief that all her physical woes
came from her "brains" and that there was some
kind of inescapable judgment in her sufferings. Her
medicine-chest had come to be one of the indispensa-
bles of her life. That she should have added morphine
to the contents seems nevertheless strangely out of keeping with the hygienic traditions of her family. Only
when she went to Boston and took a quiet room for
herself away from her family was she able to go to sleep
without morphine.

There was little done to lighten Louisa's heavy load
at this time. Her father alone of the family expressed
appreciation of what she meant to them. When Louisa
returned from Europe to find her mother ill and the
family in grief, she was greeted by one " cheerful note,
her room refurnished and much adorned by Father's
earnings." Always poor, Alcott was sincerely grateful
to his daughter whose success and fame had so outdis-
tanced his. He declared that in his lecture tours in the
West he was " riding in Louisa's chariot," though
there were many who believed that his success was due
to his own queer, stubborn, out-moded idealism.

Ultimately Louisa could not hold to her promise to

keep May abroad for a year. In November she had to send for her. Abba's poor health, the housekeeping at Orchard House, the necessity for Louisa to have some-one to stand between her and the admirers who began to come in droves to Concord, made May's help impera-tive. To her credit, May came home willingly enough. The spoilt youngest of the family responded generously at this trying time to her sister's need. The situation in the Alcott family made it necessary that either Louisa or May should take charge of the household. Only when May was at home could Louisa retire for work to her solitary room in Boston; and only when Louisa was at the helm could May be absent. When May even-tually returned to London to finish out the year that had been promised her, Louisa rented an apartment in Boston and took the whole family to the city for the winter. The obligation was one which rested heavily on both women and deterred them in their careers.

Louisa passed several listless years, from the point of view of writing. She produced only brief sketches and reminiscences and plodded along on a long-abandoned, unfinished novel. *My Boys,* the first thing she wrote after her return from Europe, contained the portrait of Ladislas Wisniewski. *Shawl-Straps,* a short but de-lightful picture of her year in Europe, followed. This little book, which Mrs. Cheney found rather too in-formal to be in the strictest good taste, was a vivid rec-ord of one of Louisa's happiest times. She first pub-lished it as a serial in Henry Ward Beecher's paper, the

Christian Union. Both Beecher and his sister, Mrs. Stowe, who was financially interested in the paper, were eager to have Louisa as a contributor. After *Shawl-Straps* they asked for another serial, and Louisa offered them the novel begun eleven years before under the title of " Success." Giving it the more modest title *Work,* Louisa proceeded to finish it in the style in which it had originally been begun. She made the Beechers pay her what she regarded as the handsome sum of three thousand dollars for the serial rights. She did not like the Beechers.

Though *Work* has little of the author's charm as a story-teller it is one of her important books. It is invaluable as biography. Christie, the heroine, goes through the same struggles as Louisa. Incidentally it is a picture of the middle-class working-woman before the war. *Work* portrays this type far better and more truthfully than Harriet Martineau's *Society in America,* usually depended upon for the purpose. Harriet Martineau's sketches were hasty observations, while Louisa's book was a voice from the people. Told in Louisa's simplest style, *Work* is a document in the form of a story. She had a paradoxical vein of fact in her, like her mystical father, who through much error and confusion strove for a method of scientific research. But in *Work* she wrote a book about, not for, adolescents. Young people passed it by. Girls, who were just beginning to go to college in large numbers when it was published, preferred *Little Women.* Had their educators been more equal to their task, they would have led them to supplement this with *Work*.

Louisa's health and spirits were at an extremely low ebb during most of this idle time. " Life always was a puzzle to me, and gets more mysterious as I go on," she complained. Again she tried new doctors and again dosed herself with drugs. " Got no sleep without morphine," reads the diary-record of October 1874. The return of May from London, brandishing a couple of laurels, helped to lighten Louisa's spirits, but did not cure her misery.

In November she took two rooms at the Bellevue, one for her writing and the other for her sister's classes. Within six or eight weeks afterwards she had completed *Eight Cousins*. It was published in January and instantly demonstrated her old popularity. The reception of *Eight Cousins* was like a popular festival.

Henry James received a copy of the book in Paris and sent a rather querulous review back to the *Nation*. " Miss Alcott," said he, " is the novelist of children, — the Thackeray, the Trollope, of the nursery and the school-room. She deals with the social questions of the child-world, and, like Thackeray and Trollope, she is a satirist. . . . We find it hard to describe our impression . . . without appearing to do injustice to the author's motives. It is evidently written in very good faith, but it strikes us as a very ill-chosen sort of entertainment to set before children. . . . The smart, satirical tone is the last one in the world to be used in describ-

LOUISA MAY ALCOTT

from a photograph made about 1885

ing to children their elders and betters and the social
mysteries that surround them. Miss Alcott seems to
have a private understanding with the youngsters she
depicts, at the expense of their pastors and masters; and
her idea of friendliness to the infant generation seems
to be, at the same time, to initiate them into the humorous view of them taken by their elders when the children are out of the room. . . . All this is both poor
entertainment and poor instruction. What children
want is the objective, as the philosophers say; it is good
for them to feel that the people and things around them
that appeal to their respect are beautiful and powerful
specimens of what they seem to be. . . . What has become of the ' Rollo ' books of our infancy and the delightful ' Franconia ' tales? "

American children, one may be sure, had changed
since Henry James's boyhood; that is, since the Civil
War. The stories of Louisa May Alcott were neither
a result of the change nor a cause of it; they were a picture of it. The " Rollo " books and the " Franconia "
tales had gone down with the beliefs which had produced them. The new children of America read *Eight
Cousins* because it mirrored the living, breathing, moving world around them.

Louisa's sister May was her inspiration for *Eight
Cousins*. She drew upon her two favourite iconoclasts,
Dr. Rimmer and Theodore Parker, for the character
of Uncle Alec. Through him she expressed her social
theories. Ideas which may be traced back to sober

Work were put into livelier form in *Eight Cousins*. A jovial, dramatic, tender story, written by Louisa with her customary charm, brought the public to this acceptance of enduring old ideals in a new form.

3

Until now Louisa Alcott had had almost no experience in society. She had plunged straight into the celebrated author's part out of the part of the poor relation. She had little skill in camaraderie though her stories seem to indicate the contrary. After meeting Helen Hunt Jackson, in whom she was greatly interested, in Newport, she wrote dryly in her diary: " Saw H. H." It had always been hard for her to make human contacts. Society in Boston was too provincial to assimilate her distinction, and except for a few odd weeks in London, Louisa Alcott knew little of meeting people on a simple social basis.

Just after the appearance of *Eight Cousins,* her health restored and her book successful, she decided in a gala mood to see the world. Her first excursion took her to Vassar College. She went to visit Maria Mitchell and see the first college for women founded in the United States. It was in February 1875. Her visit created a great sensation. Too shy to speak in public, she did not address the students in a body, and no one apparently thought of asking her to read from her works or recite one of her monologues, which she could probably have done more easily. What she did was to write in hundreds of autograph albums. Groups of students waylaid her in the corridors, armed with their albums or presenting their school-books, and demanded a line with her signature. Sitting on a laundry truck or in any convenient resting-place, Louisa amiably signed all the books that were handed her. In this impromptu fashion she met most of the girl students. " I recall her vivid personality," says one of them, " as a group of us, autograph albums in hand, waited about the laundry truck till she should write a few words for us." [1]

She was easily the idol of Vassar. " Whether then, or earlier, I am not sure, a group of us took names from ' Little Women ' and ' Little Men.' Can you fancy Vassar girls of today doing such a thing? We had our Jo, Meg, Amy, and even sweet Beth; ' Pa March,' and ' Marmee,' Laurie, John, and the Twins (in one person!) to include the whole group of particular friends. Even today, ' Meg,' ' Amy,' and ' Laurie ' are more familiar forms of address than the true names of those members of our ' March Family.' We had a group photograph taken, in costume, and sent one to Miss Alcott." [2] This was the same game which Louisa and her sisters had once played with *Pickwick Papers*. She and Anna had never ceased to be Sairy Gamp and Betsy Prig to each other. It must have caused Louisa

[1] Reminiscences of Miss Lillie Putnam Gray, of Cambridge, N. Y.
[2] Reminiscences of Miss Mary R. Botsford, Vassar, 1878.

some high heart-throbs to realize that these Vassar girls played with her works as she and her sisters had played with Dickens's novels at the same age.

Adolescent enthusiasm easily gives way to excesses. Also, the ways of shy people are sometimes hard to understand. Louisa, who could not mount the platform and speak a few friendly words to these adoring girls, could kiss any number of them out of hand — girls whom she had never seen before. "Kissed every one who asked me," she said in her diary. She looked on the episode as a joke, but was much annoyed when it was repeated more publicly and sensationally in Syracuse at the suffrage convention. In Syracuse she was all but mobbed. Her clothes torn, she had to be rescued from the girls who pursued her like mænads in the street. It was one of the worst but only one of the many trials she began about then to endure as the result of being a popular idol.

Louisa Alcott's first actual taste of society was in New York in the winter of '75 and '76. Early in the fall she arrived with her bags and pill-boxes at the old St. John's Park station in Varick Street. She was alone and she had come to the city for an indefinite stay. May had been left in charge of the household at Concord, with the present of a new saddle-horse, named for the heroine of *Eight Cousins,* for consolation. Louisa had deliberately come to New York to find inspiration and to enjoy herself.

Settling herself at some undiscoverable address, she

looked about her for society. Her memoirs refer to the place as the " Bath Hotel," but no record of any such hostelry remains. In the opinion of a contemporary resident [1] of the city, " It was probably a glorified boarding-house. Miss Alcott never felt very well-off; she had so much family." Her diary soon chronicled: " See many people, and am very gay for a country-mouse." She wrote to her father, the only member of the family who knew the city well: " So far I like New York very much, and feel so well I shall stay on till I'm tired of it. People begin to tell me how much better I look than when I came, and I have not an ache to fret over." She did stay on, taking life as she found it for about five months. Mrs. Cheney, the editor of her *Life, Letters, and Journals,* casually mentions a stay of " a few weeks." Five months was a long time in Louisa Alcott's life to be devoted to amusement. Mrs. Cheney perhaps could not believe the plain evidence set before her eyes in Louisa's diary.

She was first introduced to the suffrage and reform circles. O. B. Frothingham, one of her numerous cousins and pastor of the Unitarian Church, was the leader of a liberal and intellectual group. During an evening at the Frothinghams', Louisa was suddenly called upon to make an impromptu talk on the subject of " Conformity and Non-Conformity." Realizing that the daughter of Bronson Alcott was expected to blaze away at a moment's notice, she plunged into her maiden

[1] Mrs. Vida Croly Sidney, of Yonkers, N. Y.

speech and rather enjoyed the excitement of the unusual effort. " Didn't disgrace myself except by getting
very red and talking fast," she told Bronson.

It was a lively winter in New York. The Tilton-
Beecher suit was on everybody's tongue. Louisa took
Theodore Tilton's side, probably not so much because
of her conviction of his innocence as because of her old
dislike of the Beechers. Charles Bradlaugh, always a
public sensation, was staying in the city. Louisa went
to hear him lecture on the evening of November 26,
1875. Anthony Trollope arrived from San Francisco,
having crossed the country on the new transcontinental
railway to the great excitement of the press. Moncure
Conway had come home from Europe, to be at last
forgiven by his Virginia family for his stand on the
slavery question. He and Louisa met again as old
friends in New York. The engagement of Helen Hunt,
widowed, whom Louisa had " seen " in Newport, to
Mr. Jackson of Colorado was announced. Henry
James's article on the juvenile influence of Louisa Alcott's latest book, *Eight Cousins,* appeared in the
weekly *Nation.* The theatres were never more gay and
distracting; Central Park was crammed with fine carriages on a bright afternoon; and the political questions
and social problems of the day were enough to keep
anyone busy.

In New York, Louisa May Alcott was a literary figure
like the other leading literary people of the day; she lost
no prestige through writing for a youthful public. Mrs.

Anne Lynch Botta, who conducted the principal literary *salon* in New York in those days, invited her at once to her house. Years before, Mrs. Botta had welcomed Margaret Fuller to her circle, and later on she had entertained there Dr. William Rimmer of Boston. Largely through her introductions he had come to be employed at Cooper Union. She now reached out a motherly arm and drew Louisa Alcott into her charmed circle. At Mrs. Botta's house Louisa found awaiting her a wholly new experience: intellectual and stimulating people who welcomed her as one of themselves, without either lionizing or patronizing her. To Louisa, who was used to being treated in either one way or the other — she was never quite sure which to expect in Boston — this fellowship was one of the rare delights of a lifetime. At best she had experienced it with two or three cultivated women; now she found herself chatting with men and women of the world as if she had known them always. She found that she could be gay and irreverent and take liberties as one never did in Concord. She was humbled only when Mrs. Botta's long-haired Italian husband and his foreign guests fell into strange languages. Even then she managed to survive comfortably, seated on the sofa and joining herself to the English contingent. One could be humorous about anything in this environment, for these were trustworthy people and nothing came of it.

Her more public appearances came about through her connection with Mary Mapes Dodge, editor of *St.*

Nicholas, and Jane Cunningham Croly, also known as
" Jenny June." Through Mrs. Croly she was intro-
duced to the first woman's club organized in America
— Sorosis. Mrs. Croly's woman's club and *Little
Women* were launched in the same year. A woman of
wide interests and exceeding popularity, Mrs. Croly's
" evenings" were almost as famous as Mrs. Botta's.
Both ladies had begun their *salons* in Greenwich Village and had later transferred them to the more genteel
air of Murray Hill. In a brownstone front on Murray
Hill, Louisa Alcott assisted Mrs. Croly to receive on
New Year's Day 1876. " Helped Mrs. Croly receive
two hundred gentlemen," says her diary, for of course
only gentlemen called on that day. Louisa Alcott had
probably never met as many men as that in her whole
life.

An eyewitness of the scene, then a little girl of eight
and a member of the household, reconstructs it thus for
us: " I remember the New Year's reception very clearly.
As you probably know, it was the custom then for the
ladies of the household to stay at home on New Year's
Day and keep open house, while the gentlemen made
calls on the ladies. My mother did this for years and, I
think, was very sorry when it stopped, as she saw on
that day friends that she never saw at other times.
Punch or wine and cake were served, and the custom
fell into disrepute because the punch in many houses
grew too potent and husbands came home much the
worse for wear. My memory of my mother's punch,

tested in later years, makes me sure hers had no such evil effects.

" Every year my mother would ask four or five other ladies to receive with her, and I remember how thrilled I was when at the age of eight I was told that if Miss Alcott was well enough, she was coming this year. And she did come; and took me on her lap and was interested to know I loved her books and said she would send me her last one, — which proved to be ' Eight Cousins,' — autographed.

" Our house was a four-story brown-stone front, a little narrower than the ordinary house of the kind, as four houses had been built on three lots; but it was very deep. The back parlor where the receiving was done was a very long room. I remember a large armchair, covered with red velvet, in which the guest of honor always sat. Miss Alcott sat in the chair when she took me in her lap. It must have been a very tiring day for poor Miss Alcott, as the festivities began at noon and seldom ended before midnight. The ladies wore full evening dress, the shades were drawn, lights and candles were on, and the rooms crowded most of the time.

" I was too young to know or remember the people who came but I do know that R. H. Stoddard; E. C. Stedman, the poet; Robert Roosevelt, Theodore's uncle; A. P. Burbank, the reader and many other interesting men of the day were among the callers. So perhaps the day was stimulating for her as well as tiring." [1]

[1] Reminiscences of Mrs. Vida Croly Sidney, of Yonkers, N.Y.

One enjoys, in passing, the picture of two of the most interesting women in America: Louisa Alcott, tall, sombre-eyed until an unusually winning smile broke upon her features, fashionably gowned, ribboned, and gloved for the occasion; and beside her Jane Croly, petite, smartly dressed, animated, speaking with an English accent, and alive with energy. Around them circled crowds of well-groomed men, many of them personages of the day, paying their formal New Year's respects to the islanded ladies. It was a scene that Louisa, with her strong feeling for tableaux in life, could not fail to enjoy and remember.

Many a cold night of the winter found Louisa seated in a plush-covered seat at the theatre. She saw Clara Morris and Rose Eytinge in *The Two Orphans* and *Rose Michel* and a comedy by H. J. Byron bearing the sympathetic title of *Our Boys*. Wagner's operas were just arriving in this country. Louisa saw *Lohengrin* at the Academy of Music. On first nights at Wallack's and the Park she was an eager spectator. She kept up her lifelong illusion about the stage, never quite releasing the idea that a great actress had been lost in her. A collection of actresses' photographs always lay on her table. Her New York winter would have been a delight if it had held no other experience than her intimacy with the theatres. Summing up her visit in her diary, she wrote simply: " Enjoyed the theatres most."

What Mrs. Cheney wished to emphasize in editing the *Life, Letters, and Journals* was Louisa's deep inter-

est in the charities of New York. The interest was real
indeed, as is evidenced by Louisa's giving up Christmas Day to the feeble-minded on Randall's Island.
Turning her back on the Christmas pantomime, then
an institution in New York, and other possible gaieties,
she ferried through a foggy day across to that saddest of
islands. A benevolent Quaker lady was her companion.
They distributed gifts all of Christmas Day and returned home in the late afternoon. Louisa then found
to her dismay that her hotel had celebrated Christmas
at midday and that the help had then been allowed to
go out for their own enjoyment. Not even a cold supper was forthcoming. Incorrigible in her virtue, she
ate an apple alone and went to bed. There was some
deep association in her mind that always made Christmas a time of sacrifice rather than of merry-making.

Louisa's interest in boys led her to the refuge
known as the Newsboys' Home. The small newsboys
— very small in those days — touched her heart; but
while they awakened a maternal pity, they also suggested a fine life of adventure. The boys who often
" spent all their day's earnings in a play and a supper,
and slept in boxes or cellars after it," were the kind of
boys whom she could understand. Louisa Alcott could
not then or afterwards see all the penalties of independence for such young adventurers. She had always
longed to be a vagabond herself, though the compass
within her had always turned unerringly back to that
close family love in Concord.

One aspect of the refuge that caught her imagination was the adoption program of the people who ran it. Many of the boys were sent " out West," that miraculous place which Bostonians dreamed of, but only Bronson Alcott visited. Stories of boys who had gone " out West" and become prosperous citizens were told Louisa. So she added adoption to the other forms of social benevolence of which she especially approved.

Her New York sojourn came to an end as if it were a cycle ended. Toward the end of January, life there grew suddenly dull and uninteresting. Louisa's true home was a story-land in which she now and again lived for six or eight weeks, and all the rest of her life was spent in exile. At first it had seemed as if such vivid experiences might rival the story-land she had left, but homesickness claimed her in the end. " Find I cannot work here," she said, and took the train one day for Boston.

She tried being " a fine lady " in Boston. She took a room, unpacked her fine clothes, and began leading the same kind of life in Boston that she had led in New York. People were surprised to see Louisa Alcott about so much at clubs, receptions, theatres. But the dullness which had settled on her in New York settled again in Boston. She ended by going down to Concord with May and giving Orchard House a thorough spring cleaning. She scrubbed and scoured for a week, energetically but sadly. " It seems as if the dust of two centuries haunted the ancient mansion, and came out spring and fall in a ghostly way for us to clear up."

In June came the annual rush of admirers to Concord, who, while they annoyed her, aroused in her a sense of appreciation for what she owed them. She had in a manner come to be custodian of Louisa May Alcott. In July she made two momentous decisions. The first was to write a story which should be a sequel to *Eight Cousins,* and the second to send her sister May to Paris. In three weeks, while May at Orchard House protected her from the visiting hordes, she wrote *Rose in Bloom.* It was finished when May sailed out of the harbour, and Louisa was ready to take charge of the housekeeping.

Though her inspiration for *Eight Cousins* had been her sister May, much of her inspiration, and a good deal of her material, for the sequel, *Rose in Bloom,* came from her stay in New York. A little overladen with social theory, it exhibited at the same time a new tolerance and wisdom in the author. The love-story of Rose and Mac was the best she had done since that of Jo and Laurie in *Little Women.* Since it had to have a happy ending, she was obliged to draw less upon her experience and more upon her reason. But a reasonable love-story is permissible in a novel, if not in poetry, and may be just as convincing as a lyrical one. The episode of Rose and Mac is freshly and sanely developed from the beginning to the end. It was only a trifle sad in its implication that if the story-teller was growing a bit wiser she was also growing a bit older. She knew that if Rose was ever to fall in love with her cousin Mac she would have to fall out of love with her uncle Alec.

" Some whim had seized Mac to be shaven and shorn, and when he presented himself to welcome Rose she hardly knew him; for the shaggy hair was nicely trimmed and brushed, the cherished brown beard entirely gone, showing a well-cut mouth and handsome chin, and giving a new expression to the whole face.

" ' Are you trying to look like Keats? ' she asked . . .

" ' I am trying not to look like uncle,' answered Mac, coolly.

" ' And why, if you please? ' demanded Rose, in great surprise.

" ' Because I prefer to look like myself, and not resemble any other man, no matter how good or great he may be.'

" ' You haven't succeeded then; for you look now very much like the Young Augustus,' returned Rose, rather pleased, on the whole, to see what a finely shaped head appeared after the rough thatch was off.

. . . .

" ' Are you going *now?* ' and Rose paused in her retreat, to look back with a startled face, as he offered her a badly made pen, and opened the door for her just as Dr. Alec always did; for, in spite of himself, Mac did resemble the best of uncles.

. . . .

" ' Are you sure, Rose, — very sure? Don't let a momentary admiration blind you. I'm not a poet yet; and the best are but mortal men, you know.'

" ' It is not admiration, Mac.'

" ' Nor gratitude . . . ? '

" ' No: it is not gratitude.'

" ' Nor pity for my patience . . . ? '

" ' O Mac! Why will you be so doubtful? '

.   .   .   .

" Mac laughed too, as only a happy lover could; then, with a sudden seriousness, —

" ' Sweet Soul, — lift up your lamp, and look well before it is too late; for I'm no god, only a very faulty man.'

" ' Dear Love! I will. But I have no fear, except that you will fly too high for me to follow, because I have no wings.' "

A little lacking in the true awkwardness of girlhood, a little monotonous in the refinement of its atmosphere, *Rose in Bloom* is still one of the author's finest and wisest books. If not so good a tale as *Little Women,* in maturity and humour it stands alongside it at the head of the list.

4

Louisa Alcott said to herself at forty, in the pages of her diary: " Twenty years ago, I resolved to make the family independent if I could. That is done. Debts all paid, even the outlawed ones, and we have enough to be comfortable." And then she added this note: "Begin a new task." Her new task was a moral one: making her mother's last years as happy and comfortable as possible; for she saw that they were numbered.

This resolve motivated her life thereafter. She turned Orchard House into a more comfortable home for the invalid by putting in a furnace. For Louisa the financial rather than the climatic adventure was the great thrill. January the 1st came, and — "Paid for the furnace and all the bills!" When summer arrived, she bought a horse and a little basket-carriage and took her mother for daily drives. The following winter, despite the new furnace, she moved the family to a furnished apartment in Boston, thinking that Abba might find more interest in the city. In countless gentle and devoted ways she tried to bring comfort to the closing years of a life which she felt had been so piteously hard in the living.

Abba Alcott's illness, which incapacitated her for several years before her death, was dropsy. When Louisa sent May abroad in the fall of 1876, she shouldered knowingly the burden of her mother's sickness, but probably neither she nor May faced the idea of the end; a family accustomed to a permanent invalid seldom does. The last suffering year of Abba's life rested virtually on Louisa's shoulders alone. Bronson Alcott was frequently absent from home, and Anna was occupied with her own young family. It was a desperate trial, and only the most unswerving loyalty to her vow carried Louisa through it. Abba Alcott at last died in her daughter's arms on November 25, 1877.

5

Louisa May Alcott and her publisher, Thomas Niles, stood in their relations a good deal like Queen Elizabeth and Sir Francis Walsingham. Regal though Louisa was, Niles kept a strict rein on her policies. If the author never threw her slipper in the publisher's face, it was not because she did not want to. In fact Louisa once symbolically tried it, but the outburst did her no good; in the end, like great Elizabeth herself, she came back passively to the bit.

Thomas Niles was one of the partners and practically the sole director of Roberts Brothers, publishers. His acquaintance with Louisa Alcott began in October 1868, while negotiating terms and seeing *Little Women* through the press. Niles had at first been the friend of Bronson Alcott, who had the habit of dropping into the publisher's office as a farmer drops into a country store. To this leisurely visiting we owe *Little Women*. After Niles had become directly acquainted with Louisa, the relationship between them developed into a personal friendship.

A shrewd Yankee was Niles of Roberts Brothers, a true descendant and representative of those sharp Puritans who built the British Empire overseas. He saw no reason why ideals should not be profitable, or why they should not be presented in a way that people liked. He kept a strict watch on Louisa's style, often telling her specifically how to write, what to avoid and what to strive for, and he was full of appreciation of her hard-won successes. A quiet, unaggressive man, he was a real influence on her work and a partner in her achievements.

He watched over her health — until he gave it up in despair — her finances, her practical affairs, with the devotion of a brother. Louisa trusted him. " Don't give my address to anyone. I don't want the young ladies' notes," she wrote from Europe. It was at Mr. Niles's suggestion that his brother, living in London, took every care of Louisa while she remained there. Could it have been Mr. Niles who sent her the anonymous bouquet every day for a while after her return from abroad? He long kept a firm place in her personal life, retired and solitary though it was in the main.

After her return from New York, Louisa became restless. Her Yankee friend found her difficult. Mr. Niles wanted her to write a Philadelphia Centennial story for publication in 1876; but Louisa could feel no enthusiasm for this nationally exciting event. Mr. Niles's suggestions were sometimes a bit obvious. Of herself she rose to the inspiration of *Rose in Bloom* that year, an unquestionable success, which put Mr. Niles in his place. After this she figuratively threw the slipper and launched forth upon another scheme of her own.

Louisa had entered her middle years. She knew with the certainty that came with those years that love had irrevocably passed her by. The last ghost of the bearded lover had been laid with *Rose in Bloom*. But another ghost haunted her still. Despite all her achievement, an early unfulfilled longing still tormented her. She wanted to write a literary novel.

In the winter of 1877, revolting against destiny, Mr. Niles, and her girlish public, she shut herself up in her room at the Hotel Bellevue for as long a period as she dared leave her mother and wrote the kind of book she had dreamed of. The story was inspired by Goethe's Faust, and she called it in accordance with this fine origin *A Modern Mephistopheles*.

The plot, like that of *Moods*, dealt with an unhappy marriage. Mephistopheles, or Helwyze, and his wife, Olivia, had been estranged for many years. Into this unhallowed atmosphere two young persons were introduced as protégés of Helwyze and Olivia respectively: a young poet and a young girl. Of his cruel genius Helwyze sought to wreck their lives, and his otherwise alienated wife joined him in the enterprise. But the two young people fell in love, joined forces, and threatened to escape their evil genius. Touched by their unhappiness, Olivia relented; but Helwyze's cruel heart knew no softening. He held the young poet prisoner by his knowledge of a secret crime the latter had committed. The crime was that he had published Helwyze's poems as his own. The young wife of the poet could not understand why her husband was not free to escape from his tormentor. When she finally learned of her adored one's guilt, she died of shock and heart-break, and her child with her. The poet, grief-stricken and abased, went forth to meet his fate alone but with courage. Punishment overtook Helwyze in the form of a paralytic stroke, in which he was cared for by Olivia. The book ended with a painfully realistic picture of Helwyze's disabled condition.

It was a novel of emotion, such as Louisa might have written at the age of fifteen. *Moods,* a similar book, was a far better one. *A Modern Mephistopheles* returned to the style but not the vitality of the earlier romance. The crime was no crime at all in the world tenanted by most human beings. The half-angel, half-demon hero did not belong to a species recognized by most novel-readers. The story breathed no real feelings, no real tragedy of any kind. It was not a book for adolescents, but an adolescent book. The author had reached a period of life, sometimes and suitably called the danger-ous age, in which most people, men and women, com-mit some lesser or greater folly. *A Modern Mephis-topheles* was her middle-aged folly.

However intense the resolve with which Louisa be-gan her ambitious rebellion, it had subsided by the time the narrative was on paper; for she wrote im-mediately in her diary: " Long to write a novel, but cannot get time enough." She was back in the old familiar comfortable rut again with her dream still intact. Her disappointment was a little bitter when *A Modern Mephistopheles* met with an indifferent reception and languished on the dealers' hidden book-shelves. But when spring came, she found relief for her feelings in the shape of an allegory.

Watching her mother's life ebb, she wrote *Under the Lilacs*. It was one of her youngest and sprightliest stories, a retreat from anguish. Old Hillside memories of play with her sisters and memories of a happy May-time in Paris combined to inspire the narrative. A rather over-sentimentalized version of her mother's youth as she had always imagined it — gracious, beauti-ful, and affluent — does not seem worthy of the dying woman who sat for the picture. But Sancho, the in-gratiating French poodle, was one of those miracles of art which made Louisa Alcott great. Sancho was a real character — as real as Jo March. Clipped with a lion's mane and waving a lion's tasselled tail, he was a beauti-ful symbol of Louisa. He even underwent the severe drubbing that she had undergone and was martyred to the extent of having his splendid tail cut off. Shorn of his royal looks, he still retained all the tricks of a per-forming poodle and was able by them to support his master. Louisa had always loved allegory, since when as a child she had found comfort for the deepest sorrow in hearing *Pilgrim's Progress* read. This adorable Sancho was, I hazard, her little joke on herself and her most recent history. He was none the less a real dog, who has been known and beloved by thousands and thousands of children.

Meanwhile whatever disappointment had come to

Louisa through *A Modern Mephistopheles* had been entirely her own private affair. She owed this to Thomas Niles, who had safeguarded her reputation by publishing the story in his " No Name " series. Louisa assisted the plan by taking a naïve delight in her anonymity. Her incognito gave her an almost childish thrill. " Bean's expressman grins when he hands in the daily parcel of proof," she wrote. " Thanks for the trouble you have taken to keep the secret." Her confederate co-operated heartily in the mystery, and in truth little effort was made by anyone to dispel it. *A Modern Mephistopheles* passed as a brief excursion into folly — a book which no one but the loyal Ednah Dow Cheney ever praised.

The exact relations between Louisa Alcott and Thomas Niles, who lived and died a bachelor, were never known but were the subject of much speculation and comment. " There was some talk of a marriage between Mr. Niles and Aunt Louisa," said one of her relatives; " but I don't think there was ever anything in it." If there was ever a romance, it was a brief one. The businesslike Mr. Niles represented an alliance that was too prosaic for Louisa's high-strung temperament. Mr. Niles, too, was very kind. " There wasn't a sweeter man who walked School Street than he," said a friend after his death. But the ineradicable lesson Louisa had learned at home was that such a man is negligible. Her relationship with her publisher con-

tinued along lines of mutual friendship and helpful-
ness as long as they lived.

6

When Louisa sent May to Paris to study art, it was
with the expectation that May would there see her
friend Ladislas Wisniewski; and it so happened. The
young Pole seemingly lived on in her emotions though
she had purged them by writing a long novel and one
short story about him. She had corresponded with him
up to the Franco-Prussian War, when he had been lost
for a time; after this interruption they had corresponded
again. Whether for value received or out of generosity,
she had sent money to him through her publishers.
Laddie still lived in her thoughts as a youth whom she
must shield and protect. Finally she sent May to him
as her personal envoy.

With eagerness she awaited news of their first meeting. It followed promptly upon May's arrival. At once
Ladislas constituted himself May's cicerone, doing for
her the things he had once done for Louisa. He escorted her to the museums and to the shops, helping
her to spend the money that Louisa sent her. May was
no simple and naïve shopper like Louisa, satisfied with
a showy hat. She was a connoisseur in antiques and a
fastidious dresser. Shopping with her was not the gay
and jesting pastime Ladislas had found it to be with her
sister. No return of the other delightful idyll came

with this contact. It was merely a pleasant social formality.

Ladislas was living in an apartment in Paris with his mother; and he was ten years older now. May's brief references to him in her letters soon changed to interest in his mother and the Wisniewski family affairs. There was no hint that the personality which had been projected by Louisa's imagination into a million girlish hearts was still vivid, or that it had ever shown its brilliance to others besides Louisa. In a short time all mention of him was crowded out of May's letters by more exciting people and events. Paris, which had been so long for Louisa the city of Ladislas Wisniewski, became instead the city of May Alcott.

7

It is hard to believe that the fever of migration had not yet burned itself out in the Alcott family. In the midst of the anxious and troubled crisis of 1877 they moved on again. With Mrs. Alcott fatally ill and Louisa too infirm to walk, they once more indulged in one of the old picnics. Orchard House in Lexington Road was exchanged for a residence in Main Street. This change, one may add, was the last migration of the restless Alcott genius. Although they spent winters in Boston, the family dæmon at last came to rest in this new, and fifth, Concord domicile.

Yet for twenty years it had lived steadily in Orchard House. Here was accumulated a rich store of family memories. To this house Louisa and her parents had returned after Lizzie's death and Anna's engagement. The tumble-down dwelling had been restored by Bronson Alcott's own hands to the last fireplace, bookcase, and clothes-horse. Louisa had written her first novel here. In the parlour Alcott, Emerson, Samuel May, and Elizabeth Peabody had discussed the problems of the universe. Up and down these stairs Louisa and May Alcott had gone over and over on their bended knees, ardently pursuing the ritual of spring and fall cleaning. Here were all the various improvements into which Louisa's hard-earned money had gone to make the family comfortable. Upstairs were the little room to which Anna's fatherless boys had returned and May's room, where those fine copies of Flaxman had been flung so carelessly upon the woodwork by the occupant while she dreamed of a great future. Above this still was the attic chamber, Louisa's Spartan den, where she had written so many of the books that had made her famous. All was forsaken in the blind way in which people obey an unconscious dæmon. With Abba scarcely able to endure the moving, and Louisa seriously ailing, they departed forth out of Orchard House. Fortune had been kind to them for long, but now grief and sorrow impended, and the old family reaction to trouble, the pattern to flee, revived. The drive to escape, where no escape was possible, was one of the fundamental Alcott impulses. Abba Alcott died ten days after they left Orchard House.

The old Thoreau house to which they moved had only recently fallen on the market. It was a dignified white house under the elms, a more elegant place in a more resplendent location than the old brown house on the hillside. " You will have the amusement of people looking in upon you occasionally," May wrote from Paris, " and some little passing in the street to vary the scene from Wheeler crossing to the barn and Moore's cows coming home at night." The price of the new homestead was $4,500, toward which Louisa Alcott contributed $2,500. The remainder was paid by Anna out of the small estate her husband had left her. It became the permanent Alcott homestead, though the name, the Thoreau house, continued to cling to it permanently.

The reason Louisa gave herself for this remove was: " Nan wants a house of her own, now that the lads are growing up." How much necessity there was in this wish may be judged by the circumstances. Louisa's nephews, fifteen and twelve, were certainly growing up, but her younger sister had just announced her intention of living abroad. In all too short a time Abba's place in Orchard House would be left vacant. The house would then be large enough for those who remained; and the lack of a barn, which had recently become a hardship, was easily remedied. In fact Louisa had long planned to build that barn, as she had written to her father from New York. There was no real reason for transferring the roots of this remarkable family from Orchard House to a strange spot except the awakening of the Orestean curse which had long lain dormant.

The transference in fact proved impossible. When all the furniture had been removed and the house was an echoing emptiness, it was still, to the exclusion of the new Thoreau house, the home of the Alcotts. People still came in carriages or on the newfangled bicycles to look at the bare windows of the home of the popular author. Louisa herself was known to drive by and with an odd kind of detachment point it out as the home of Louisa May Alcott. Strangers bought the house and occupied it; but such was their respect for the past that they preserved all its features intact including May Alcott's pencil sketches on the woodwork. The spirit of the family kept vigil there until in the course of time the place came back to it wholly and entirely. Mellow with the memories of the twenty years of her life spent there, the house remains to this day a faithful and true memorial of Louisa May Alcott.

CHAPTER XI

Head of the Family

THE THOREAU house was at first a haven and an inspiration to Louisa. She wrote two stories about it — *Under the Lilacs* and *Jack and Jill*. Although she gave the house to Anna and always called it " Anna's house," she herself felt unusually at home there. She returned voluntarily from her Boston hotel more often than usual, while she noted, for the first time and to her surprise, that living at home was "cheaper."

The place was replete with memories of Henry Thoreau, who next to Emerson had been the Alcotts' main friend in Concord. There his mother and sister had lived while he occupied the little hut on Walden Pond built by himself and Bronson Alcott. There he had died in 1862, when Louisa had written her best and most melodious poem in his memory.

       " The wisdom of a just content,"
which

      " Made one small spot a continent,"

met her restless spirit on the threshold of its new life in this quietly beautiful white house.

With her elder sister, Louisa led a pleasantly ordered life. Anna Pratt knew how to spread an atmosphere of peace and comfort around her. She was an instinctive home-maker. In Orchard House, where everyone had talked about the housekeeping, no one had done it; this was the paradoxical régime of the simple life. When Anna had married John Pratt she had emancipated herself from transcendental housekeeping. In Main Street Anna kept house. Louisa continued as always to be the head of the family, but her sister created a home for them. It was the first time such a state of things had ever existed in the domestic history of the Alcotts.

Louisa Alcott found herself after all these years of living in Concord making friends in the village. Her visitors were no longer limited to transient celebrity-hunters and hero-worshippers. Now when she stepped into her little phaeton and took the reins in her hand, it was not always to turn Rosa's head toward the woods, but sometimes to drive around paying visits in the town. She brought guests home from Boston to lunch; on one particular occasion she brought Frances Hodgson Burnett and Mary Mapes Dodge, just up from New York. " Most agreeable women," said Louisa, complacently. This little event would have been inconceivable at Orchard House.

Another agreeable change came to the family at this time. Bronson Alcott seemed to acquire all at once the respect and regard of his community. For years Alcott had found his sole appreciators in the West; or so he had believed. Inexplicably, when he was seventy-nine, this seemed to change. " Father comes to honor in his old age," Louisa noted in her diary. The door of the Thoreau house opened increasingly often to admit Alcott's admirers, and the little phaeton was frequently requisitioned to show his guests about Concord.

A gradual equanimity of spirits came to pass in Louisa. The uneasy and rebellious spirit of " Apple Slump " was at rest, reposing at last under the sod of Sleepy Hollow. Louisa grew reconciled to her loss; to May's exile; to Concord. Anna Pratt had always been pro-Concord, and her serene influence had its chance at last in her sister's life. In spite of occasional illnesses, Louisa now led a calm and contented existence in Concord, yielding more and more to the peaceful charm of the place. The village became for her synonymous with harmony. If she could have maintained this atmosphere her life might have been greatly prolonged.

2

Louisa was reconciled to May's absence by the realization that May had achieved all that she had set forth to accomplish. After a belated start, she had marvellously caught up with the dreams of her youth. " Regrets that these opportunities have come so late in her life," mentioned in Abba's diary, were rather the re-

MAY ALCOTT NIERIKER

Courtesy of Little, Brown and Company

grets of a doting mother. May's full and happy days left her little time for regrets.

May Alcott belonged to the post-Civil-War generation. Though not so much younger in years than Louisa, she nevertheless tenanted a wholly different world. The war had made the difference. Louisa was well started in life before the conflict broke out, while May still lingered in the late adolescent stage. A more realistic generation emerged at the end, — a generation for whom old traditions had been sharply broken off. To this new group May Alcott belonged. Within its ranks the young and talented strove for guide-posts in place of those they had lost. Louisa, though in close contact with this generation, did not understand it. She had occasional fleeting glimpses of its aims, however. Vistas were opened to her during the winter she spent in New York that led her to the wish to be more helpful to May. After this she sent May to Paris.

Louisa Alcott's sister has been little known in this country. Her exceptional character has been but slightly appreciated. The American painter Will Low, who was in France at the same time as May Alcott, was asked about a possible acquaintance with her and replied: " There were two Inns at Grez, Chevillon's, where we, the Stevensons and our band stayed, and the other, whose name I forget, and which I fancy was considered the most respectable, though that may be because it was slightly more expensive. Coming from Concord, whose philosophy would I am sure have been tried by the general disorder at Chevillon's, Miss Alcott may have preferred the second of these places." Not knowing May, he guessed wrong. May Alcott would under no circumstances have missed the atmosphere at Chevillon's; in fact, that was where she stayed. Daniel Chester French, who knew May better, said: "She was unhampered by the heritage of that New England conscience which ruled Louisa with a rod of iron."

The domestic atmosphere in the Alcott house had a different effect on the three Alcott daughters. Louisa revolted against all housework as tyranny and fled it whenever possible. Anna's revolution took the form of always insisting on orderly comfort around her. May developed out of it a simple and true bohemian life of her own. She was perfectly happy in a little room " so small it can't help but be cozy," with her " little duds, new Delft vases, etc.," scattered around and with a hot muffin for tea, " toasted before a blazing fire, held there stuck onto a gilded dagger for a fork, and washed down by a cup of nice cocoa." May was a natural simple liver. Her tastes were not therefore always for the inexpensive, as her hard-working sister Louisa realized. She liked clothes, and her " little duds," which ranged from a cream-coloured stuffed owl to " a golden saint in a coffin five feet long, which caused much interest at the Custom House," were genuine of their kind and tolerably costly. Like Bronson Alcott, who would, and did, sell his soul for books, May was something of a collector. She could never in her life have done her work in the bare attic in which Louisa wrote her stories.

But no Alcott was without a social conscience. There is a passage in *Little Women* in which Jo and Amy argue about reformers. Amy says: " I don't like reformers," and Jo replies: " I do like them . . . for, in spite of the laughing, the world would never get on without them." Yet even May could not escape the stamp of the family. Assisted by the local philanthropist William Munroe, she opened the co-operative Art Center in Concord, a studio which flourished splendidly for several seasons. In Paris she formed one of a group of women art students who organized and conducted their own studio. Her dreams, too, ran along this line. " When I become rich and great," she wrote, " I shall found a school for indigent artists and aspiring young students, as Rosa Bonheur has done in Paris for girls under twenty years of age. I have still thirty more years to work in and think, if I am spared, that I may do something in that time."

May and her father were the most distinguished-looking members of the family. May had caught her father's high-bred air. Her features were irregular, but her golden-brown hair fell in natural curls below her waist — frequently worn so in Paris — and her tall figure moved with a rhythmic grace. She was strong and athletic, rowing a boat and riding a horse with ease and skill. Of her body it was said that she would have been more beautiful without clothes than with them. This was not the kind of praise that meant much in Concord and Boston; a smaller nose and a less determined chin would have won her more favour in the home town. But there were still those who called May pretty, so beautiful was her hair, so charming her manner — when she wished to make it so — and so graceful her general aspect and impression.

The American Miss Alcott, with her long curls down her back, was a striking figure in Paris between 1877 and 1879. May's residence in Paris began in the autumn of 1876. She had spent a couple of winters in London studying drawing with Rowbotham and copying Turners in the National Gallery so well that Ruskin had noticed her work and praised it. Her journey to Paris, however, she viewed as her final dedication to art. " She was sober and sad," said Louisa, recalling her departure, " not gay as before; and seemed to feel that this might be a longer voyage than we knew. The last view I had of her was standing alone in the long blue cloak waving her hand to us, smiling with wet eyes till out of sight." In Paris and Grez she worked with tremendous industry, and within a year after she had left off copying Turners in London she had arrived at the point of having her own work exhibited in the Paris Salon. Evidence of her further progress in the technique of painting is seen in the acceptance of her second picture by the Salon. At the end of two years

she was earning by the sale of her paintings a mention-
able income. May's sympathies and tastes were with
the rising impressionist group, which she would probably have joined had she lived longer. She and Mary
Cassatt were personal friends, but it was not merely for
this reason that she entered so passionately into the differences between Miss Cassatt with the Academicians
of Paris. May came out uniformly on the side of the
bold and original in art. Her own special interest in
painting the Negro was decidedly unconventional at
that time.

Needless to say, she had not come thus far without
some stumbling and fumbling about love and marriage.
But May faced up her natural desire with a realism and
frankness unusual in her age. The adolescent mood,
set forth by Louisa in her Rose's words: " I've been
gay, then sad, then busy, and now I'm simply happy.
I don't know why, but seem to be waiting for what is
to come next," was no longer hers; though it was considered in those days the only possible mood in which
a respectable woman of any age could regard marriage.
But May had long since outgrown this youthful and
unconscious brooding. Bronson Alcott, who knew his
children well, said of May that she had what he called
" a clear understanding." One of the problems of her
life which she directly faced was trying to work out the
relation of her work to marriage.

As May grew up, two definite paths had been demonstrated before her — the path of ambition and the path

of love. They were clearly set forth by the examples of her sisters: Louisa had chosen ambition, and Anna had chosen love. Each of the two older sisters had in her way a strong influence upon her. With the scales weighted in this fashion first on one side and then on the other, May worried through a good many years, unmarried, gaining the reputation of a flirt, and not accomplishing anything noteworthy in her art. Finally the urgent need to solve her own problems — that of her career and that of her personal life — led her to the new frontier of Paris.

The relation between May Alcott and Dr. Rimmer has always been and must perhaps always remain an interesting mystery. How much or how little they meant to each other is an unsolved riddle, much like the ever-interesting riddle of Charlotte Brontë and Professor Héger. Family annals briefly state that May was Rimmer's pupil and that Louisa paid her tuition. But one cannot fail to observe how important was his influence. Her virile yet delicate drawing, developed in France, was in Rimmer's peculiar and excellent style. May Alcott might with time have developed into a distinguished etcher like Mary Cassatt. Settling down in France, she chose for a home Meudon, near Paris, associated with the memory of the royal French family and hence with the memory of Rimmer's royal ancestry. Here she accomplished, though in contradiction to Rimmer's theory, the realization of her dream of an artist's career. For Dr. Rimmer had always stressed the fatal effect of marriage on a woman's talent. It was one of his well-known and grumbling complaints about his women pupils that "as soon as they get somewhere, they marry." In one way or another Dr. Rimmer's teachings and theories pursued her.

May's marriage took place in the spring of 1878 in London. She had met Ernest Nieriker several months before this, either in Grez, or Paris, or London whither she had gone in the previous autumn as a better place to sell pictures. He was a German, engaged in business, who had lived variously in Switzerland, Paris, and London. May was thirty-eight and Nieriker was but twenty-two. Though the marriage had been vaguely expected by the Alcott family, it took place rather suddenly. The young German was on the point of being shifted by his firm to a new post, either in Paris or in Russia. To prevent a separation, the couple were hastily married at a London registry office.

Unlike Louisa, May had not shrunk from marriage with a man many years her junior. She followed beauty consistently and wooed it in all its forms and love was for her another form of beauty. In Nieriker she had met a belated offshoot of the German romantic movement, one who played the tenderest of old folk-melodies on his violin and who, with his open collar, tumbled curls, and soulful eyes, resembled the youthful portraits of Goethe and Schiller. To May he looked like the love-god: " Large hazel eyes, a handsome nose with proud nostrils and as beautiful a mouth as I ever saw,

almost perfect in form . . . a firm, decided chin . . .
throat . . . round and white as a woman's." Could a
woman who had won happiness through beauty then
turn her back upon a career dedicated to its worship?
May's non-Puritan nature answered emphatically no.

Once married, the couple went from London to
Havre, where they lingered for a week considering
which post to accept, the one in Paris or the one in Russia. With May's art ambitions weighting the scale, it was
apparently an easy choice for them to go to Paris. She
spent a blissfully happy week in Nieriker's company.
" The lonely artistic life that once satisfied me seems the
most dreary in the world," she wrote. " Our tastes are
so congenial it seems impossible that we shall ever
clash " — but why prolong this sanguine note from the
midst of a honeymoon? The imagination lingers, however, over the thought of how nearly May Alcott's life
came to including a journey to Russia in 1878.

They took the little apartment at Meudon and settled
themselves in it. " I am going to combine painting and
family, and show that it is a possibility if *let alone,*" she
wrote. " In America this cannot be done, but foreign
life is so simple and free, we can live for our own comfort, not for company." " I never mean to have a house,
or many belongings," she added, " but lead the delightfully free life I do now, with no society to bother me,
and nothing to prevent my carrying out my aims and
in succeeding in something before I die." Quite naturally she accomplished more than she had ever done

during the next two years, in which she lived quietly with her husband in their charmed little apartment. Her canvases multiplied at the dealers and at exhibitions. She added writing to her other activities, for like all of the Alcotts she could write, easily and well. She exhibited her second Salon picture, published her first book, and had a baby all in one year of her brave, high-spirited, and briefly fulfilled life.

May Alcott's child was born in November 1879, and she herself died seven weeks later. At first she seemed to make a normal recovery. Her child, a healthy little daughter, she named Louisa May, shortened soon to *Lulu* by the German relatives. Then, after a little time, came a disturbing change in her condition. Only her mother-in-law and a midwife were in charge; physicians were not summoned. She drifted into a stupor in which she lay for several baffling weeks, sinking deeper and deeper all the while into unconsciousness. May died, and was buried beneath a French gravestone in the outskirts of Paris.

There are indications that despondency and depression beyond what might have been expected of her condition weighed upon her in the last weeks. They are seen in the minute directions she left to be followed in case of her death: pitiful suggestions that her casket should be a virginal white, that her body should be laid in the old Montrouge cemetery, and that her baby should be sent to her sister Louisa. These revelations of the mood in which she faced her woman's ordeal suggest that she had lost some of the high courage which had carried her thus far and which she now more than ever needed.

In the absence of positive data about their earlier relations, one should not attribute too much significance perhaps to the fact that Dr. Rimmer's death preceded May Alcott's by a very short time. But about two months before her child was born, she received the news that Rimmer had died at his daughter's home near Boston. One cannot but be surprised at the absence of all mention in her diary and letters of this widely mourned event. Unless May was singularly ungrateful — and she certainly was not that — she could scarcely have failed to feel sorrow for the loss of a great teacher. It is more probable that she felt a deep and special grief, unsettling in her state and estranging to her household, and that this accounted for her pre-parturient depression.

The sudden ending of May Alcott's life in Paris was a great loss and a deep tragedy. Her talents were late in developing. She might never have become a painter like Mary Cassatt or a writer like Louisa Alcott. But there was a gallantry of the spirit in her which combined with her talents and ideals to make her one of America's pioneer women. It is a public loss that the legend of her life should be so little known to the women who came after her. The restoration of her memory should be a pleasant and an interesting task for the young generation which first discovers her.

Louisa's opinion of her youngest sister changed several times in the passage of years. For a long time she did not believe in May's talent, as her portrayal of Amy in *Little Women* as the perfect lady shows. This was not merely because Louisa herself " had no soul for Art," as she was willing to confess, but partly because May's art career was so slow in maturing. Louisa clung to the idea that her sister was chiefly interested in " Society." Only gradually did the older sister discover that the other needed help on the serious side of her life. Finally, her sketch of May in *My Girls* gave the first expression of her really new attitude toward May as a fellow-worker. " B is an artist, loving beauty more than anything in the world; ready to go cold and hungry, shabby and lonely, if she can only see, study, and try to create the loveliness she worships." " A more deeply gratified young woman it would be hard to find than B," the sketch continued, " as she now plans the studio she is to open soon, and the happy independent life she plans to lead in it." Her generous delight in May's success, her belief in it, were in part her conviction that the younger woman, too, had settled down to living for her career. Then her sister's incredible marriage followed and she was obliged to open the question of May all over again.

Louisa found it hard to forgive May for her marriage. It had not been easy to forgive her sister Anna for marrying ordinarily many years before. That May should have consented to a union with a man sixteen years her junior was a betrayal of something deep within her: the rooted family pride she had inherited from her mother. Her realization of the strength of the temptation did not make her any easier on the culprit; she had been separated forever from her Laddie by a slighter difference of years. " Sent her a thousand dollars as a gift, and all good wishes for the new life." May was to understand that nothing more would follow. Nothing did! The only money the absentee received from home after her marriage was a small sum from her father. Though Louisa was sometimes almost won over by May's ardent and appealing descriptions of her happy life, she had no great faith in it. " May it last! " she said. She entered only the most conventional remarks about the expected baby in her journal. " May sits happily sewing baby-clothes in Paris. Enjoyed fitting out a box of dainty things to send her. Even lonely old spinsters take an interest in babies." May earnestly begged Louisa to come and be with her during her confinement; but Louisa, who at first planned to go, was in the end prevented by ill health. Thus, in spiritual distance and bewilderment, without understanding or real forgiveness of her sister, she was overtaken by May's tragic end.

" I cannot make it true that our May is dead, lying far away in a strange grave, leaving a husband and child whom we have never seen." She could, indeed, never make May seem true again — never wholly perceive the motives that had led her out into those far frontiers where in silence, loneliness, and mystery she had perished. Louisa's grief was always to be weighted by her unanswered query.

3

In the snowy midwinter previous Louisa Alcott had turned her back on the house in Main Street and gone to Boston, to write. "At the Bellevue in my little room writing," she noted; "begin an art novel, with May's romance for its thread." This, for one who had always made a jest of her lack of knowledge of art, was a strange choice of subject. At the end of a month, feeling "rather used up," she packed her unfinished manuscript and went back to the quiet and repose of her sister's house. The summer months, punctuated by tennis and boyish society, passed idly over the arrested novel, and by the time August had come and gone, it had been transformed into *Jack and Jill*. The art novel, whether it was an attempt in the manner of *The Marble Faun* or something in a more modern manner, was lost to history.

Jack and Jill was Louisa's only story about Concord. She was accustomed to say that Concord had no inspiration for her and that this was the reason for her numerous flights to Boston. "Its sleepy life and sad memories are not the material out of which to weave bright, healthy stories for children," she told a reporter from the New York *Tribune*. To this habitual attitude the summer of 1879 was the one notable and delightful exception. " Harmony Village " was, to be sure, not the old Concord of Orchard House days, but the new Concord of the Thoreau-house environment. " Jack and Jill are right out of our own little circle," she told Mrs. Dodge. The background was the simple village life with which Anna Pratt's family made a naturally close contact. The circle to which her young nephews belonged gave Louisa characters and atmosphere for her tale. " Young people much interested in the story," she noted, " and all want to ' go in.' I shall have a hornet's nest about me if all are not *angels*." The sole remnant of the art novel that survived in the transformation was the romantic thread of love borrowed from May Alcott's life. *Jack and Jill* was another instance of what Henry James declared Louisa Alcott so culpably wrote for children: a novel.

The Concord idyll centred on a little French-Canadian girl and a little American boy who loved each other. The story was developed from a sled upset which happened with more or less serious consequences. When Louisa's sister Anna broke her leg after a year in the new house, Louisa nursed her and took her place in the household. With her usual inventiveness she turned this experience into fiction. Her family as always supplied her with characters: in this case her widowed sister and her two nephews provided the cast. Little Jill as a French-Canadian represented the far-away sister in Paris without introducing a false note in New England. " She looked like a brilliant little flower. . . . The French blood in her veins gave her color, warmth, and grace, which were very charming." Louisa was, in imitation of her sister May, thoroughly under the spell of the French myth. The mothers of Jack and Jill were their only parents; there was no Mr. Minot, no Mr. Pecq. This was again a story of a matriarchate, like *Little Women*. Jill's long-drawn-out illness gave the opportunity for the serious moral note inherent in Louisa's philosophy. Jill is usually said to be Louisa's impression of the little invalid girl she had taught in Beacon Street many years before. But she seldom turned so far back for models. Jill was more probably the joint portrait of the three Alcott sisters, May, Anna, and Louisa, combining the youth and romance of the one, the sad accident of the other, and the temperament of the third. Nothing was easier for Louisa's intrinsic magic than to turn grown-ups into children.

But the boys in *Jack and Jill* were drawn from living boys of the same age. She dipped into the Concord "gang" with an unfettered hand. The boys in the story were those she found around her in the summer of 1879. Truthfully she said of her characters: " The nearer I keep to nature, the better the work is." While she shuffled the cards somewhat, many of the portraits were kept very close to nature. Jack and Frank Minot were done by the simple method of holding the mirror up to the real characters of Jack and Fred Pratt, her nephews: Jack Minot, lovable and petted; Fred Minot, independent and serious. " Minot " was an old Pratt family name. Ellsworth Devens, wearing the slightly rougher description of " Ed Devlin," stepped into the story just off a bypath of Concord. This gentle boy was the son of abolitionist parents associated with Bronson Alcott and Frank Sanborn in the old fighting days of the fifties. He was the same age as Louisa Alcott's eldest nephew and was known as a most angelic boy. Another of the Harmony Village lads, " Ral " Evans, was probably Francis Elwell, the sculptor. Other Concord boys, less easy to trace, perhaps, but surely in the story, were the two Simmons brothers, Edward, afterwards the artist, and William, the Bangor, Maine, physician. Boys in *Jack and Jill* came out of the richness of that village life to make name and fame for themselves elsewhere. For, notwithstanding all that Louisa Alcott did to fashion her boys as ordinary fellows, they persisted in developing talent and ambition under her pen. These were of course the kind of boys that she knew.

That second summer in the Thoreau house carried Louisa swiftly and inevitably onward toward the age of forty-seven. Perhaps a sudden shadow, as sometimes happens, fell across the path of her bright summer, carrying a vague forecast of autumn and winter. One naturally seizes then upon the nearest bright object that dispels the ominous shade. Louisa Alcott found the brightest objects around her to be boys of school age. If she responded to the stimulus with more warmth than a woman of her age usually accords to boys of theirs, it was her peculiar expression of her momentary need. As far back as *Little Men,* she had written of herself: " I really don't know which I like best, writing or boys "; and Nat, she had added, " who had never heard anything like this before, really did not know whether Mother Bhaer was a trifle crazy, or the most delightful woman he had ever met." Long after the period of *Little Men* she was still attractive to boys and attracted by them.

That was the summer when croquet and *Pinafore* reigned in Concord. Boys of that summer long afterwards kept alive in memory a vivid picture of Louisa May Alcott running across the croquet-ground waving her wig on her mallet. She trolled with the lads in her tuneless voice snatches of the Gilbert and Sullivan opera or joined in the chorus which surrounded her nephew as he played the accompaniment on the piano. She did a good deal of laughing that summer, for, in spite of occasional bouts of illness and some worries concerning May, it was a season unusually free from trouble. But as all her bright seasons seemed short and fatally destined to end in sorrow, this one was no exception. On August 8, 1879, Ellsworth Devens, the gentle Concord boy, died after a brief illness. Her affection for the youth is frankly expressed in the dedication of *Jack and Jill* and in the beautiful character she represented him by in the book. As so often after a heart-breaking loss, she started immediately upon a story after his death.

Jack and Jill contains her apologia for putting so many deaths in children's stories. It was an old habit beginning with John Sulie's death in *Hospital Sketches* and had aroused some criticism by its persistence. It emanated in fact from a long, long memory of the masterly voice of Dickens, who was responsible for a great many deaths, not always sentimental, in nineteenth-century fiction. Ed Devlin's funeral had the serene epic mood Louisa knew so well how to impart to the occasion, creating an atmosphere of sympathy and mourning out of her own reserves of feeling without the aid of conventional religion or piety. It was one of her naïve triumphs as a writer for her times. Her simple eulogy: " Good and happy, — the two things we all long for and so few of us truly are, — this he was," gave to the memory of an obscure lad a tender lasting glow. By a somewhat touching slip of the pen she mentioned the dead boy in one place by his true name.

She kneaded reforms into her plots as she kneaded in parties and games, and the young reader was never sure which was coming next. In *Jack and Jill* the chief social reform was temperance, because she thought it the best to introduce in a story about boys. Louisa Alcott was very much under the spell of the vivid personality of Frances E. Willard, then in the heyday of her popularity and influence. It was not Miss Willard's particular organization, however, that she used in her story but an older international society for men and boys. Co-education, then much debated, also played a prominent part in the book. Education in general had become more and more the acknowledged aim of the author. " Fathers and mothers tell me they use my books as helps for themselves," she said; " so now and then I slip in a page for them."

Louisa Alcott was coming more and more to wear the mantle of the rejected Bronson and to spread his teachings abroad through the land. " School is the child's world while he is there." — " There is plenty to learn outside of school-houses." — " Busy minds must be fed, but not crammed." — " The adolescent is ready for college in one way, but not in another. Hard work is no preparation for four years of still harder study." — " The girls read aloud a good deal . . . they could stop and ask questions as they went along, so that they understood what they read, which is half the secret." — " Lessons, exercise, and various sorts of homework made an agreeable change." — " People shook their heads, and said it was wasting time." — " Education is *the* problem of our times."

Some of the charm of *Jack and Jill* was the spirit of democracy in Harmony Village. The children were good Americans; their May-day parties, Washington's Birthday parties, and October Fairs were genial gatherings for all the town. This was the view of Concord which Louisa took for one brief happy summer before May's death. It made *Jack and Jill* a permanently popular book with American readers.

4

During the World War, which threw the emotions of fear, anxiety, and insecurity into high relief, recently developed theories of the emotional nature of man received strong confirmation from the facts then observed. The knowledge of mental and nervous disorders was afterwards greatly increased. There is no reason to suppose that similarly intense disturbances of the emotional life did not arise in the American Civil War. The term shell-shock which was used in the World War to cover a great variety of nervous disorders had not then been invented, but the phenomenon itself was well demonstrated in the after lives of the veterans of the North and the South.

It was some form of shock to which Louisa May Alcott succumbed as a hospital nurse in 1862. Mrs. Cheney says of her illness: "The severe attack of fever which drove her from her post left her with shattered nerves and weakened constitution, and she never again knew the fulness of life and health which she had before." Louisa said herself of the experience: "I was never ill before, and never well afterwards." This was not merely fever, for of a fever germ one quickly dies or recovers. But an injury to the deep-lying nervous complexes on which the personality is based is a serious affliction from which one recovers perhaps after a long period of time; perhaps never.

It was an injury to which Louisa must have had a

predisposition from childhood, but which she might have escaped without the supervention of her Civil War experience. The latter was an accident, but greater or lesser accidents are a part of the finite life. It is necessary to prepare for them all in good season, and the season is in childhood. The child who, like Louisa Alcott, is brought up on fairy-tales, is hovered over and kissed when asleep, is taught to believe in good and evil, who is moreover not accustomed to regular hours or regular food, is, to this extent at least, ill prepared for the accidents of life. Add to this the presence of something called " temper " in the family environment, the belief in it as the individual's sacred privilege, and an atmosphere is created that unfits a sensitive child for handling his own nervous crises. All this was true in Louisa Alcott's case. She who did so much for children by her stories may do them the further service of warning parents by her life.

After that time in Washington, she was the victim of constantly recurring and more or less serious illnesses. While her attacks may have been hysterical, her suffering was none the less intense and real. She suffered from neuralgia so severely that she had to carry her arm at times in a sling. Her aching bones made comfort in any position impossible. A delicate throat caused the complete loss of her voice for months at a time; insomnia plagued her persistently; and digestive troubles fastened their stubborn hold on her. Her life lost enormously in joy and activity through her constant wearing invalidism, which, in spite of physicians and treatments, committed her to pain and debility. After paying a visit to the doctor she wrote: " Dr. S. told me I was better than she ever dreamed I could be, and need not worry." Yet the misery and depression continued and the symptoms returned to harass and oppress her.

Her second extreme illness after the Washington experience came after the publication of *Little Women*. The strain of success, the compression of new attitudes, new relations, new responsibilities, within the rather fixed limits of her life, brought on a repetition of her former illness. A similarly severe attack befell her during the last weeks of her mother's life. " I overdid and was very ill, — in danger of my life for a week." It was at such crucial emotional moments that her health most dangerously failed her. But there was far too much illness in her best of health, as is evidenced by many slight circumstances. During her winter in New York, when she seemed to be most happy and busy, she was receiving her mail at her doctor's address; and she could only promise Mrs. Croly in advance of her appearance at the New Year's reception that she " would come if she was well enough." As the years accumulated and sorrows and misfortunes came faster, her resistance grew less and her frailty increased. Health was her constant preoccupation and, for all that, she was not able to maintain it. Increasingly her life became a medley of complaints and treatments.

Her real trouble was, she kept automatically repeating in her diary, her nerves. She never gave any closer description of her ailment than this. It was taken for granted that the Alcotts should suffer from nerves; and they did. Abba Alcott was especially a sufferer in this way. The day was yet far distant when the diagnosis and treatment of such troubles would begin to make their phenomenal progress. In the light of what is now known, however, it is supposable that Louisa Alcott's case might have been helped by more understanding.

As everyone has his own particular type of insanity, provided he ever goes insane, Louisa May Alcott had hers. While she was never in any danger of actually going insane (except perhaps for a moment during the war), she approximated her type more nearly than the average healthy person. She existed in a permanent borderland of hysteria, in which, as the author of *Moods* demonstrated all too well, periods of elevation over which she seemed to have no control alternated with equally unrestrained periods of depression. Anyone who has read Louisa's diaries knows these opposite moods of hers as they are expressed there.

A devout believer in authorship from inspiration, in the " divine afflatus," she would have considered it heresy to try to control her writing dæmon in any way. Her " vortex," the mood in which she wrote her novels, was a kind of mania. " Can't work slowly. The thing possesses me and I must obey till it's done." When in this state, she could continue writing fourteen to sixteen hours a day for weeks at a stretch, almost without food or sleep, sustained only by that mysterious sense of excitement and the sweet vision before her. Without physical comfort in her environment, bent over her knee as a desk, she continued until the wave of madness in which her book was written was finished.

Her moods of depression, which followed, were prolonged and severe. The sleeplessness which accompanied the writing of her books remained to torture her then in the form of insomnia. In one of her early attacks of this kind, that which followed the death of her sister Elizabeth, she contemplated suicide. Later on, in her early forties, when her family responsibilities were especially heavy, she suffered such agony from sleeplessness that she fell to using morphine. Yet she did not commit suicide, and she never became a morphine addict. She was always sufficiently aware of her nervous weakness to control it in part and her native common sense and humour came to her rescue. When she said of a character in *Rose in Bloom* that she " was a capital patient because she never died and never got well " she gave expression to an observation made on herself.

Given Louisa Alcott's predisposition to illness and her adventurous nature, one would expect to find her eager to try all the healing arts and devices of her time. This she almost methodically did. She was like a president or king in having a constant medical attendant. From the general practitioners, she proceeded to specialists; and from specialists she went on to special healers, such as homœopathists and osteopathists. Pioneer women physicians found her a most encouraging patron, but she passed restlessly back and forth between them and men physicians. After trying all the schools of medicine, she placed her faith mainly in homœopathy. The best-known names of physicians in Boston are associated with hers: Dr. Hewett's, Dr. Woesselheft's, Dr. Greene's. The famous Dr. Bowditch, who was a pioneer in the use of psychological means for the treatment of physical ills, was at one time her physician. Dr. Eli Miller, no doubt a homœopathist, treated her in New York. It seems as if among so many at least one might have been found able to help her; but among them all there seems to have been not one who gave her any aid beyond the ordinary routine treatment.

At one stage of her troubles she was impelled to try mental healing as such, but she did not consider the experiment successful and withdrew very definitely from further attempts of the kind. In a letter published in the *Woman's Journal* of Boston, she wrote: " Writer's cramp and over-worked brain were the ills I tried to mitigate by the new cure, of which marvellous accounts were given me. With a very earnest desire to make a fair trial, I took about thirty treatments, finding it a very agreeable and interesting experience up to a certain point. No effect was felt except sleepiness for the first few times; then mesmeric sensations occasionally came, sunshine in the head, a sense of walking on the air, and slight trances, when it was impossible to stir for a few moments. Much agreeable conversation, the society of an agreeable person, and the hope that ' springs eternal in the human breast ' made these earlier weeks very pleasant. . . . But when thirty treatments left the arm no better and the head much worse, I dared lose no more time, and returned to the homeopathy and massage from which I had been lured by the hope of finding a short and easy way to undo the overwork of twenty years."

The revelations of this letter started one of the few public controversies of Louisa's life. Readers assumed that her letter referred to Christian Science, then fairly new in Boston, though Christian Science was not mentioned in it by name. In fact, the Christian Scientists discovered upon investigation that the particular healer Louisa had employed was not actually one of them. They contented themselves with a published statement to this effect, and the tempest which had for a short time raged about Miss Alcott and Mrs. Eddy died down.

Like Margaret Fuller, who experimented with mesmerism in Paris, and Elizabeth Barrett Browning, who tried spiritualism in Florence, Louisa Alcott felt that she had to test the power of occult influences to help her. Also like them she was not strongly enough interested in what she found to remain influenced for any length of time. Adventurous and imaginative natures seldom fail at some time in their lives to make such little excursions into the land of all-helpful magic. But those who carry with them an inevitable edge of intellect seldom fail to cut their way promptly out of the unreal maze. Louisa Alcott had that kind of intellect.

5

When her health failed her most, she fell back on short stories. " I can do two a day," she said, " and keep house between times." In this way she turned out hundreds of them which appeared in magazines and were then assembled under the titles of *Camp and Fireside Stories, Spinning-Wheel Stories, Proverb Stories, Silver Pitchers,* and so on. Popular as they were, they were not her best work. Her love-stories were not real and she could not make history live. Only those sketches which were based on details of her own family life succeeded. " A Modern Cinderella," the story of her sister's courtship and marriage, " Transcendental Wild Oats," the story of Fruitlands, and " My Boys," containing the personal sketch of Ladislas Wisniewski, were the successful exceptions.

Louisa began writing her short stories at sixteen, contributing them to the weekly papers which travelled by mail-coach all the way out to the wilds of Wisconsin and the prairies of Kansas. The weekly newspaper was the forerunner of the monthly magazine, which first flourished after railway trains had become general. Her short-story audience grew up with the country. The prosperity of the magazines was her prosperity. They kept her in steady funds with which to pay doc-

tors' bills and school tuition and buy food and clothes
for the consanguineous Alcotts.

Her early development in the magazine field coin-
cided with the growth of special magazines for children.
Elegant and nevertheless childlike, *St. Nicholas* flourished surpassingly among them. Without Louisa May
Alcott, *St. Nicholas* might not have existed; without
Mary Mapes Dodge, its editor, it certainly would not.
The combination of such talents had much to do with
the success of a periodical that wrote a chapter in
American culture. Louisa Alcott and Mrs. Dodge were
in a way repeating the partnership that Louisa Alcott
and Thomas Niles formerly had had. The friendship
was a refreshing influence in Louisa's life and work.
All of her books beginning with *Eight Cousins* appeared serially in the pages of the *St. Nicholas,* where
young girls — now old ladies who remember the event
with pride — eagerly and ecstatically read them.

One of her early children's stories, called " Cupid
and Chow-Chow," was unusually and deservedly popular; Louisa created in it a small hero modelled on her
young nephew John Pratt. The plot, the romance and
adventures of a little boy and girl, was a prelude to *Jack
and Jill.* Incidentally, it took a rather humorous view
of the woman's-rights movement, which was not helped
any by the fact that Louisa called the fictitious suffragist
of her story " Mrs. Susan." All this caused some misunderstanding and annoyance at the suffrage front,

until it was eventually wiped out by a letter of explanation from the author.

One need only read Louisa Alcott's description of Cupid to detect in it a resemblance to another well-known juvenile character. " Mamma began it by calling her rosy, dimpled, year-old baby Cupid, and as he grew up the name became more and more appropriate, for the pretty boy loved everyone, everyone loved him, and he made those around him fond of one another, like a regular little god of love. . . . Our Cupid's costume was modernized out of regard to the prejudices of society . . . he was gorgeous to behold in small buckled shoes, purple silk hose, black velvet knickerbockers, and jacket with a lace collar, which, with his yellow hair cut straight across the forehead and falling in long, curling love-locks behind, made him look like an old picture of a young cavalier." The pictures which accompanied the text were likewise a forecast of the famous juvenile character to follow. When *Little Lord Fauntleroy* swept the country a few years later, producing a multitude of suffering small boys in black velvet suits and long curling locks, it was partly because Louisa Alcott's " Cupid and Chow-Chow " had first set the style.

When Louisa wrote her story, the age of æstheticism had not yet come in America. That age followed upon the visit of Oscar Wilde to this country. Mrs. Frances Hodgson Burnett wrote *Little Lord Fauntleroy* at the height of the tide, when the passion for ornament and refinement had escaped all bounds, and her story was the purest single expression of the era to which it belonged. Louisa Alcott's " Cupid " was written for a public which still allowed common sense to correct the extremes of romance. The whole point of her story was that the love-god developed into a little boy — a point that was missed by her friend, Mrs. Burnett, when she took up the legend later to develop it in her own style.

6

There was never any real doubt about Louisa May Alcott's place in the woman-suffrage movement. She occupied it by every law of her ancestry and nature. Puritan, philanthropist, and abolitionist in her background, she was not due to stand aside from a sound and reasonable social reform. She was a strong advocate of woman suffrage.

But she came to it along the New England way rather than along the Seneca Falls way. She was originally much more interested in the economic position of women than in their political position. This was partly the result of living in a highly industrialized state and in taking part in the economic struggle. Like the woman who knew, when a tile from a roof fell on her head, that the roof was defective, Louisa knew that there was something faulty in the economic position of woman. She was, in the years before the war, more interested in the question of woman's work and the remuneration for it than in the question of woman suffrage. " I am so busy just now proving ' woman's right to labor,' " she once said, " that I have no time to help prove ' woman's right to vote.' "

Later, however, she was won over to being an active, even a militant, supporter of political rights for her sex. She took part in a national suffrage convention, gave her money to the cause, and became one of the editors of a suffrage magazine. Her alliance with the suffragists dragged her out of her retirement, as it dragged many another shrinking though less gifted woman out in those days. It was one thing for Louisa Alcott to write suffrage editorials and articles and it was quite another for her to lead a procession through the streets of Concord and to demand of the august chairman of a public meeting that he pay respect to the woman-suffrage delegates by giving them seats. For thus far in the dust and heat of the arena did Louisa advance. She brought her personal influence to bear on Thomas Niles to cause him to publish a history of the suffrage movement; " for," she wrote belligerently, " we are going to win in time, and the friend of literary ladies ought to be also the friend of women generally." Mr. Niles published the book. Looking about for more worlds to conquer, she discovered that she could vote in Concord by paying her poll-tax. She paid the tax and voted; so did her sister Anna; so did five other women whom she called out to exercise this privilege.

Louisa's dislike of the kitchen was the kind which

was popularly expected of a suffragist, but which all suffragists were not able to feel. "We don't like the kitchen department," she announced, "and our tastes and gifts lie in other directions." Long before her income had been increased by *Little Women,* she had begun to employ maids in the kitchen. This only led to troubles with "help," so that the black incubus of the kitchen continued to haunt her. She never became entirely emancipated from it, except at intervals when she fled to hotels or lived with her sister in the Thoreau house. Her crowning act of revenge against this domestic department was the purchase of a seashore cottage "without the curse of a kitchen to spoil it." Here she dreamed that by a single act she had wiped out the hateful institution.

The only kitchen she ever loved was the tin kitchen in the attic in which she kept her manuscripts. Yet she loved another one too: the kitchen of her fantasy around which she spun so many delightful stories of food and cooking. The woman who immerses herself in the actual *materia* of the kitchen is not the one who writes the best stories about it.

A catalogue of the reforms in which Louisa Alcott was at one time or another interested would be surprisingly long and modern. Her ideas concerning education, temperance, housing, and prison reform could still be used to point the way toward improvements in those fields today. She always stopped on the sane side of all reforms because her main interest, when every-thing was said and done, was in story-telling.

Her attitude toward the poor was one of sympathy with the problems of genteel poverty. For, in spite of the hardships the Alcotts had suffered, this was the only kind of poverty that she had known. The implacable poverty which grasps and distrains the vitals had never touched her. Her sympathy remained with the " silent poor "; it never crossed the bridge to the actual poor beyond.

But no one equalled her as a teacher of democracy in daily life, of happiness in small things, and of the in-spiration in the simple affections.

CHAPTER XII

Early Frost

THE LATE flowering of Bronson Alcott formed one of the most dramatic of the many dramatic episodes in the Alcott family. At the age of eighty he blossomed out as a poet. He had continued year after year, winter after winter, making his lecture tours through the West and the South, and nothing except extreme illness or death in the family had interrupted them. His six or seven months on tour came round as regularly as the equinoxes and the seasons. His tall figure, cape, and snowy locks were familiar from Kansas to Florida. As he grew older and more the accustomed thing on his route, his welcome seemed not to wane but to increase. He attributed this with his usual grace and humility to Louisa and *Little Women*. But in all justice to Louisa's great fame, it appears that Alcott really owed his success as a lecturer to his own personality. His magnetism and vitality created for him his own public aside from his daughter's. It was a public which continually grew and would not allow his retirement, and when he did retire, followed him in part to Concord. Perhaps they were right. Alcott should not have retired. He made his last trip in his eighty-second year and, completing it in sound and regular health, gave up all itinerant lecturing for the future.

A School of Philosophy had been planned for him in Concord. It had been opened tentatively in the vacant rooms of Orchard House in the summer of '79. The following summer a glorified barn was erected on the hillside above the orchard and the flourishing academy installed there. Four or five hundred people made the journey to Concord each summer to sit at the octogenarian's feet. William T. Harris, Alcott's great friend and afterwards his biographer, rented Orchard House and eventually bought it, in order to insure the site of the school. He was one of a number of devoted friends who gave money and otherwise supported it. The success of the summer academy was assured from the start; Alcott enjoyed in it in the eve of life a great personal triumph. Though Emerson was associated with him, it was Alcott and not Emerson whom the American pilgrims came primarily to visit.

Some people seem to come very late to the climax of their lives. For much more than a third of a century Emerson had been the first gentleman of Concord;

hordes of travellers had sought out the town only to see him. Then Louisa May Alcott had been for a great many years the main objective of the sightseers. But now the town teemed with people who came to see and hear Bronson Alcott, last to achieve this eminence. Physically and mentally he bore the onslaught well and the visitors went forth again well pleased with the latest god of Concord.

In the glow of rejuvenating success the philosopher revived his interest in building. It was twenty or thirty years since he had built an addition or restored an old house. Now he fell to and added a wing to his daughter's house in Main Street. It cost him the sum total of his last year's earnings, but it gave him a much-prized library. Besides, that was the first thing that every successful celebrity in Concord did: add a wing to his house; unfortunately success sometimes ran up into too many wings. In his pleasant, well-lighted, harmoniously added quarters, Alcott met his staff and counsellors of the School of Philosophy. Wearing his white Panama and carrying his gold-headed cane, he issued forth on fine summer mornings to stride up to the Gothic barn and deliver his fifty or more lectures. The little family phaeton was in active service showing ardent visitors around historic Concord.

These were gala days for the octogenarian. Every summer Concord was turned into a festival in his honour. But the festival passed when winter came. Alcott, in his long cloak and his beaver hat, was seen striding

AMOS BRONSON ALCOTT

from a photograph made about 1880
Courtesy of Little, Brown and Company

along the snowy paths of Concord for the first time in
many years. When at home he read in his new library
and — at last! — wrote poetry. He had always been the
greatest lover of poetry in America, but beyond occasional verses had never attempted the art himself. At
the age of eighty he luxuriated in writing poems. They
were in theme curiously interesting variations on his
lectures, which had frequently been characterizations
of people whom he knew. Some of the sonnets had the
same subjects as his lectures: Emerson, Margaret Fuller,
Thoreau. A little volume of these poems, *Sonnets and
Canzonets,* published after his first winter spent thus
in Concord, were the proud vindication of his personal
life. For with him, as with all the Alcotts, writing was
the supreme aim of existence.

It was generally said of Alcott that he only learned to
write well in his old age. This was not exactly true, for
he was writing excellent prose essays on education before his marriage. But even his oldest and best friends,
Emerson and Sanborn, did not seem to know this or else
they had forgotten it. Marriage had been the avalanche
that covered the young educational writer from view.
The pressure of that union wiped out a promising
young man's career. The transmutation of his talent in
his daughters, especially Louisa, gave the first evidence
that the hidden stream had not been lost, but had come
to the surface again. Its later revival in his own poetry
was a revelation and an astonishment to all.

During his brief Indian summer Alcott and his

daughter Louisa were fellow-celebrities. Louisa was no longer the sole lion of the family. The tall and stately couple went about together; no one now snubbed Alcott while inviting Louisa to dinner, as Henry James, Senior, had done in his day. They became an accustomed sight in public. Walt Whitman visited Concord about this time and a reception was given him, concerning which he noted: " My friend A. B. Alcott and his daughter Louisa were there early." Another interesting glimpse of them occurs in the diary of a less famous person, a young Concord girl: " One evening we went to a reception at the studio of Daniel French. . . . When the carriage came for us it was occupied by Mr. Alcott and Louisa. The latter immediately became absorbed in chatting with my aunt, which left Mr. Alcott to amuse himself with a young girl like myself. He was as courteous as though I had been a queen. . . . He certainly won my heart from that day." Still another comment, made by Louisa herself, throws light on the way in which she and her father trod the path of fame together in those days. " She once spoke of herself," says a friend, " as one destined to fill niches, being a wife to her father, a husband to her sister, a mother to her little niece." It was rather a pleasant season in both their careers when they received in common applause for much that they had in common accomplished.

Though Louisa's financial contribution to her father's life at this time was slight (she gave almost no money to the School of Philosophy; the school was the peculiar labour of Alcott's friends and except for small donations paid its own way), she rendered it its meed of respect and admiration. With a kind of wonderment she set down in her diary: " Father comes to honor in his old age." What seems a bit cruel is that she never attended any of the various lectures, least of all those of the family philosopher. But it must be remembered that her health was not good and her energy limited; and also that she received at home hundreds of calls from the students. Her pride in the venture was un-bounded and it started, after a long period of inactivity, the impulse to write another book. *Jo's Boys* was based on the School of Philosophy, and made of Louisa one of its most far-reaching influences.

Once again we hark back to that psychiatric quirk in Louisa Alcott's mind which did so much to shape her life. Frank Stearns understood her better than anyone else when he said: " She honored her father and lived more for him than for anybody else, including herself." He is, I believe, the only one of Louisa Alcott's biogra-phers who admits this. Most of them are agreed in thinking that the difference between them was real and fundamental. This was actually true only in so far as their superficial relations were concerned. In the depths of the affections which lie beyond the reach of words Louisa was her father's most adoring daughter. She loved him maternally, rejoicing in the late expres-sion of his talent and taking as much delight in her father's success as in her own. Louisa never put her father in a work of fiction except most casually; but in her poems, which, though her poorest work, expressed her feelings more than did her prose, she often wrote of him. So, by some process of reasoning or by some special sense of his own, Stearns divined that Louisa cared more for her father than for anybody else, however definitely she sometimes acted and spoke to the contrary. Her condition was not unlike that of a patient who was dismissed on parole from a mental hospital with this instruction to the guardian: " Her only trouble is that she thinks she has no money. She has plenty. See that she pays her bills." Louisa Alcott had within herself a buried treasure, so deeply hidden that only the rare person saw it; and last of all she herself. She could never draw consciously upon her riches because she did not know that she had them. It was a psychiatric quirk of no slight significance, for, of all diseases of the soul, the lie about love is the worst. Louisa suffered from it all her life long, finding to the end no complete release. Indeed, the older she grew, the more sickness-ridden, and the more battered by other kinds of suffering, the less she seemed to know herself. Fleeing from self-knowledge, she was lost.

In the spring of 1882 Emerson died. Alcott's friend for so many years, his comrade in so many ventures, the companion of his mind, of his ideas, of his life — Emerson had been all this and more. Their platonic love had been the mainspring of Alcott's life for almost fifty years. When it suddenly ceased, he was smitten at the heart as a rabbit is smitten by a shot. Louisa wrote: " Emerson held his hand, looking up at the tall, sorry old man, and saying, with that smile of love that has been Father's sunshine for so many years, ' *You* are very well, — keep so, keep so.' " She stood with her father beside Emerson's open grave; and as he staggered back and harshly clutched the shoulder of a small boy near him, she cried out sharply: " Pa, you are hurting Georgie." The shock of the loss for her father was greater than Louisa could possibly grasp.

During the Summer School of Philosophy, Alcott seemed to be himself again. But when fall arrived and with it the accustomed time for him to take the long trail for the West with his old comrades of the road, the cords of his life broke. Louisa was called home from her hotel in Boston by the news that her father had had a stroke of apoplexy.

Alcott did not immediately die. He lived on for six years, and not always as an invalid. He still attended the sessions of the summer school, which continued to exist as long as it had his mere presence to sustain it. There were periods of comparative well-being when he read, received visits, or drove out with Louisa. Then the progressive illness had its turn again. In the Thoreau house his sick-bed stood in the library that he had built. Here he wasted by degrees to his end — a slow tragedy which Louisa with her Cassandra temperament had described like a prophecy in *A Modern*

273

Mephistopheles. Thus he lived on in the shadow to the age of eighty-nine.

2

The expression of Louisa Alcott's face changed as she grew older. The rather proud and determined look of the thirties gave place to a more tolerant and patient mien in the fifties. " My pictures are never successes," she once said. " When I don't look like the tragic muse, I look like a smoky relic of the great Boston Fire." Her colouring was never clear or brilliant, but to make up for that she had excellent features. Some who knew her in her fifties have called her beautiful. She was an ornament to a *salon,* though she seldom graced one. People who recall her in her latter years mostly agree in describing a street impression. " She would come through the posts that shut off Louisburg Square," says one who remembers her,[1] " where as a girl I used to wait to see her, wearing a cloak, — always a cloak, — and a bonnet. Her hair was soft and wavy in the bonnet." Alas, the hair was what Louisa called her top-knot.

Her clothes with the years took on much elegance. But she never became one of those women who know how to wear clothes. There was always a bit of the hoyden left over beneath the rich lace and velvet and sealskin which formed her dress in later years. " Miss Alcott had a friend in New York," says her dressmaker

[1] Mrs. Walter Taussig, of New York City.

of those days,[1] " who sent her many lovely dresses and coats. Her friend was a little stouter than she was, so everything had to be refitted and sometimes other changes made. That is how I knew Miss Alcott well. She was a little above the medium height, forty-two bust, hips in proportion, well set up and weighing I should think a hundred and forty or fifty pounds. She was a very lovely person to meet and work for; not fussy and very considerate of others. She cared very little for clothes and thought them a bother." So even in her most affluent years Louisa spent comparatively little money on her clothes. The habit of wearing other people's made-over garments was a habit that clung to her from childhood. Aside from reasons of economy and of long custom, the practice must have been congenial to her nature. She never rebelled against it as did her sister May. But very elegant she seemed to the outside world in her successful years, even though her elegance was not accounted for on her personal bills.

An unsocial woman, she nevertheless took the greatest joy in any party that meant theatricals. Games, charades, and picnics always enlisted her help, furnishing that curtain of formality through which she most easily met people. By this means she enjoyed the company of the young, with whom she was most at home. " Mother and Aunt Louisa were always getting up plays," said one of her nephews. " People were always laughing when Aunt Louisa was around; for without

[1] Mrs. Frank Pierce, of Concord, Mass.

trying to be entertaining, she could keep her guests and callers in a roar." Her sense of humour was stimulated by an audience. But it was much like her elegant clothes and cheerful fantasies, worn for the benefit of other people. In her hours of solitude she too often found that she had already exhausted her resources in that line.

As she grew older, responsibility became almost a fetish with her. She could neither refuse it nor make terms with it. Her only answer was to accept it utterly. She was literally what Alcott's sonnet called her: " Duty's faithful child." She persisted in the merciless strain, though fate seemed to be playing an unceasing game with her, piling burden upon burden, adding service to service, as if to try whether implacable fact might not shake her adherence to the ideal she had chosen. In one of her stories she describes a childhood fantasy of a god called " Kitty-Mouse," a contradictory creature to which the child sacrificed her most precious and adored toys. It was as if in her life, too, duty assumed for her this same monstrously contradictory shape, demanding of her still the same blind and obedient worship.

This contrary god presided over her relation to her family. Her devotion to them is the crown of her life-history. She lived for them. But she could not live with them. As often as she attempted to settle down in a Concord house or a hired apartment in Boston, as often did she flee from the Alcotts' home-life; the attempt

LOUISA MAY ALCOTT

with James E. Murdock—her last photograph

always ended in her departure for the hotel or for some rented place where she could be alone. It was a sad and perverse sequence. " There was something *einzig* about her," said a critic, " that made her restless and unhappy when she was tied to other people, though she could and did work herself to death for them." Perhaps the influence of her father's example played a large part in this restless life of hers. Perhaps, in spite of her great fame abroad, she always felt herself a " scrub " at home, as she said of her representatives in her stories. Perhaps she had only elected a trade that requires a great deal of loneliness, and, owning neither compromise nor guile, she did not know how to obtain it in the midst of a family.

Though Louisa fought her moral battles alone, she was fain to call in help in the battle for physical health. She clung to her doctors more than most patients do. The New York *Nation's* obituary said of her when she died: " Miss Alcott seems to have had no intimate friends outside her own family." The exceptions to this were her friendships with her doctors, most of them, naturally, women, with whom her sickness brought her in intimate contact. But when the need for their professional aid ceased, the intimacy evaporated. There was no place in Louisa Alcott's hardriding life for the pleasures of mere friendship.

In her last years a persistent weakness caused her to lean more heavily than usual on Dr. Rhoda Lawrence. Dr. Lawrence was a homœopathic physician and a pioneer woman after Louisa's own heart. She had been a teacher, a telegraph operator, and a masseuse; and in middle life she had studied medicine and taken a medical degree. When Louisa knew her, she was in charge of a children's clinic in Roxbury, near Boston. This busy life might have been lifted bodily out of Louisa's early novel *Work,* a novel founded on the author's own experience. It is easy to see that Louisa Alcott's and Rhoda Lawrence's careers had much in common that might form the basis of an unusual friendship.

More as friends than as doctor and patient, the two spent summer vacations together at Princeton, near the old site of Fruitlands. I believe that Rhoda Lawrence came to stand in the same relation to Louisa as once did Abba Alcott, inheriting the aura of idealization with which Louisa had always endowed her mother's image. Later still, when illness had more greatly weakened her, Louisa went to live at Dr. Lawrence's home in Roxbury. There she had the care of a sanitarium and sank back thankfully into the rest and peace which had come to be all that she asked of life. Ardent in all her feelings, she worshipped her kind doctor and called her last retreat in Dr. Lawrence's house " Saint's Rest."

3

A roster of the Alcott family in those days — unfortunately a group photograph of them all does not seem to exist — would have included individuals of three generations. As a household they were still set apart from the rest of the world. Only in one youth of the third generation, who early showed exogamous tendencies, did the family stockade show signs of yielding. They were still Alcotts, down to the children's children, holding fast to the centripetal family.

"May left me her little daughter for my own," said Louisa to Mrs. Dodge. It did not seem strange to Louisa at all that the child should be thus sent away from its father and given to its maternal relatives. Little Louisa May Nieriker arrived in Concord in the fall of 1881. During the whole preceding year Louisa had dreamed about her and planned for her, hoping that here at last was the tie for which all her life she had been waiting. She was prepared to give her life to her baby. A perfectly appointed nursery and a trained nursery-governess were in readiness for the child's arrival, though something simpler might have promised less responsibility for Louisa and better prospects for the wish-dream. In the sequel, she spent more time running after the governesses than she spent running after the infant. Not thus is the thwarted maternal instinct, released rather late in life, really satisfied. Louisa's relations with her child were warm at times and at times perfunctory. "Wish I were stronger, so that I might take all the care of her," she said. "We seem to understand each other, but my nerves make me impatient and noise wears upon me." And so the tie from which she had hoped so much was not created in the child's infancy and never developed the strength that was prefigured in her dream.

Louisa's generosity to her small relatives was unstinted. She supplied her little nephews not only with such necessities as warm suits and copper-toed shoes, but also with every proper toy that bloomed in the market. They had the first bicycles and cameras in Concord; the best musical instruments, and of course many books. She made investments early for their schooling; although, strange to say, she took no interest in college for them. It was difficult for Louisa Alcott to see the need of college training when she had never missed having anything of the kind in her own life. Both youths entered the employ of Roberts Brothers under the tutelage of Mr. Niles and began their careers by packing vast cases of their aunt's books for shipment. Louisa, held back by ill health and trying to finish her last book, found herself impatiently urged by her enthusiastic young nephew to " swamp the book-room with ' Jo's Boys.' " Still staunch to her standards, she managed in all ways to be the perfect source and fount of the family's blessings.

With this knowledge she might well have satisfied her maternal longings. But it did not content her. The adoption of the younger of her two nephews, John Sewall Pratt, as her own son and the change of his name to John Sewall Pratt Alcott points to a hungry striving for a happiness she had lost. She was much shattered in health when she took this step in 1887. The reason she gave for it was that some doubt existed concerning her right to bequeath the copyright on her books to collateral descendants. Though she had already so bequeathed it, she now feared that her family was not safe unless one of her nephews was legally adopted. This fearfulness she imposed upon the entire family. It was only a mechanical and legal adoption after all, for she had already grown to be an isolated invalid in Dunreath Place.

The elder of the two nephews was married about this time. Breaking out of the family stockade he had gone forth and found himself a wife. He had presented her, gentle, blonde, and wide-eyed, to the great lions at home. With what awe did the young guest survey the distinguished Aunt Louisa, then still handsome in black velvet and lace, and the famous Bronson, last of the transcendentalists! But later, when the marriage took place, Louisa and Bronson were too ill to attend it.

The houses which formed the background of these last events in Louisa Alcott's life were several. Louisa bought or rented several different residences in these last years. There were the cottage at Nonquit, a house in Pinckney Street, an apartment in Boylston Street, and a house in Louisburg Square. Louisburg Square, on the slope of Beacon Hill, was the symbol of all that she desired to give to her family. In the autumn the leaves fell sedately there; in the winter the snows piled high around the black-branching elms. A spirit of ancient dignity brooded over the square. One could easily picture the ancient senators sitting around on the stoops waiting for the barbarians to come and pluck their beards. From Louisburg Square a young man just entering society could very suitably go forth in search of a wife. Another could wear a top hat without shame. A little girl with a refined governess could play quietly in the square. And a stricken old man who had spent his early life combating everything in Boston that Louisburg Square represented could pass his last unconscious and indifferent days there attended by trained nurses. But Louisa Alcott herself lived hardly at all in Louisburg Square.

The tranquil domestic genius of Louisa's sister Anna held the Louisburg Square household together. It was a large house, and when Louisa moved into it in the fall of 1885, she thought she would find under its capacious roof a room of her own with her family. But she fled from the attempt soon; and, being much too ill now to live alone in her old room at the Bellevue, she retired to Dr. Lawrence's house in Roxbury. Thenceforth she kept the Louisburg Square house as her official residence, though she only paid visits and received her mail there.

Out of such flights into loneliness, restlessness, and emptiness she made her rich, breathing, ardent stories of home.

4

The Alcott family were what is known among the orthodox as without religious affiliations. With the exception of Abba Alcott, who clung to her old King's Chapel faith through all the heterodox vicissitudes to which her marriage exposed her, the family had no orthodox church. It was not that they were antagonistic to religious ideas; these ideas did not penetrate to them in any vital form. They had been filtered through the personality of Bronson Alcott. He had all his life taken a great interest in religions — from Buddha to Alexander Campbell in the South and Mrs. Eddy in the North — but it was an investigator's interest. His rather comprehensive and well-known studies antedated and possibly stimulated William James's *Varieties of Religious Experience*.

In Louisa Alcott the family indifference was especially manifested. She tried in her sensitive adolescence to " get " religious. " I had an early run in the woods before the dew was off the grass. The moss was like velvet, and as I ran under the arches of yellow and red leaves I sang for joy, my heart was so bright and the world so beautiful. . . . A very strange and solemn feeling came over me as I stood there. . . . It seemed as if I *felt* God as I never did before, and I prayed in my heart that I might keep that happy sense of nearness all my life." When in deep trouble after her sister Lizzie's death, she went to Theodore Parker's church. But her final attitude was one not so much of ignorance as of innocence. When she published *Hospital Sketches,* someone remarked on the lack of religious atmosphere in the scenes of suffering and death depicted. Louisa replied to the criticism, but was not affected by it. The lack of religious spirit shown in *Hospital Sketches* was the prelude to the same lack in all of her stories to the very last. There was no indication in a lifetime of stories that she was aware there was any omission.

After *Hospital Sketches* the issue was not raised again by the public. When she ceased to be a New England author and became an American author, her readers no longer took any note of the matter. Her popularity was nevertheless the product of a church-going era and a church-going public. The explanation must be the evident sincerity which she brought to her work; she never wrote about any belief that she did not ardently hold. She never turned in her personal life to a religious group outside the familiar churches of her environment. No cult, no quasi-religion, no exotic doctrine was adopted to fill a loss which she never felt. A sincere personal philosophy (much as she hated the word!) was all that she lived by and all that she had to give others in her books. Even the most conventional religious people are willing to accept this if it contains no antagonism to their own beliefs. Thus did Louisa Alcott become one of the finest bequests of transcendentalism to the succeeding age.

The Alcotts, in poverty and deprivation, contributed

riches to American letters. Louisa Alcott published about thirty-five books, and Bronson Alcott published eight or ten. May, after years of painting, turned at last to writing and put forth her own little volume. Anna, the eldest, published, with a preface, her own and Louisa's plays. The letters and diaries of the whole family have found their way much into print, adding to the memoirs of the life of their age and proving that an Alcott needed only a pen to produce a literary style. What American letters owe to this remarkable family is an interesting and unestimated total debt. They are a considerable part of our American cultural heritage.

5

Miraculously Louisa Alcott could lift herself out of sickness and sorrow into that upper empyrean of the mind where only light and enchantment prevailed. The magic of her stories continued. She grew anxious with time lest her power should forsake her. " Don't let me *prose*," she wrote to Mrs. Dodge. " If I seem to be declining and falling into it, pull me up, and I'll try to prance as of old." But children still watched as of old for Louisa Alcott's stories and could have told her that her fear was unnecessary. Even to the last of them, her stories kept up their cheerfulness. Her perspicacious remark, made early in life, applied at the end as well: " I have had lots of troubles; so I wrote jolly tales."

Her last long story was *Jo's Boys*. This book was begun in the solitude of a hotel room, but was interrupted by her father's stroke and was not completed for six years. There were months when she did not touch it. Part of the time she could write only one or two hours a day. Yet, handicapped as cruelly as this while writing the story, she dealt out in it with the same sure hand the unfailing charm and cheerfulness.

The material of *Jo's Boys* was taken as usual from the author's family life. Laurence College, rather a nondescript institution based on the School of Philosophy, was easily acceptable in an age when colleges multiplied so fast that one was scarcely established before — as the saying ran — " they were cutting poles for another one." The book contains a chapter of intimate autobiography — the harassments and plagues of the life of an author. It is Louisa Alcott's confession of the thorns and prickles that fame had brought to her. The characters in the book are those of *Little Men* grown up to the threshold of manhood, finding work, travelling abroad, falling in love, falling into disaster. The old beloved Meg, Jo, Amy, Laurie, and Professor Bhaer make once more, and for the last time, their appearance. Woman suffrage, temperance, co-education flaunt their banners once more across the lively pages of Louisa's narrative. Perhaps affection for old characters as much as anything else makes the book dear to readers, for it admits faults not present in earlier stories. Some confusion in it was probably due to the broken, interrupted way in which the story was written. The appearance of Meg Brooke's second daughter, Josie, causes no little surprise in the reader who remembers that John Brooke died in *Little Men* leaving only one daughter behind. The second daughter, of course, is little Lulu Nieriker, May Alcott's child, then the youngest member of the Alcott household. Whether the spirited and ambitious Josie corresponded at all in character to her original is impossible to know. She seems a more probable portrait of Louisa Alcott's own youth than of her little namesake. One never saw the little half-German niece in any of her stories. The actual lineaments of the actual Alcotts were now disappearing behind a slowly falling curtain.

Louisa had a sad premonition that her saga was nearing its end. "It is a strong temptation," she wrote, "to close the present tale with an earthquake which should engulf Plumfield and its environs so deeply in the bowels of the earth that no youthful Schliemann could ever find a vestige of it. But as that somewhat melodramatic conclusion might shock my gentle readers, I will refrain." Later she added this further aside to her readers: "And now, having endeavored to suit every one by many weddings, few deaths, and as much prosperity as the eternal fitness of things will permit, let the music stop, the lights die out, and the curtain fall forever on the March family." Yet the writer was so essentially of the prima-donna type that readers might well have hoped for several last appearances.

But *Jo's Boys* proved in fact to be her last long story.

She began almost immediately after *Jo's Boys* was finished a book which was called "Mrs. Gay's Summer School." Her pleasant idea for a plot was "to have some city girls and boys go to an old farmhouse, and dress and live as in the old times, and learn the good, thrifty old ways, with adventures and fun thrown in." As this story never grew to more than two chapters, what promised to be a happy tale of early New England life and manners was never finished for readers.

While she was still painfully plodding through *Jo's Boys,* Louisa began to collect the stories she had written for very young children in a series of little volumes. These she dedicated to her niece and called *Lulu's Library.* "Old ladies come to this twaddle when they can do nothing else," she wrote Thomas Niles. But the stories were not twaddle; there was many a bright bit of imagination scattered through them. *Lulu's Library* also included a reprint of *Flower Fables,* written at sixteen and so inferior as youthful work to the blood-and-thunder dramas she wrote with Anna at the same age that one speculates at times on the power of Anna's lost literary talent.

An error of judgment due to failing health, perhaps, but very hard to forgive was her treatment of her beloved first-born, *Moods,* in 1882. Of this first novel her nephew said: "Had she not been so generous with her time, she would doubtless have written more novels. As it was, she was always waiting for an opportunity to write another book like ' Moods,' which I believe to have been her favorite." This makes it the harder to pardon the vagary which caused her to transform it twenty years after it had been published. Anyone who seeks a copy of *Moods* in the antiquarians' shops today will find it with a copyright date either of 1865 or of 1882. If he finds it with the second date, he will have to keep on searching if he wants to read *Moods* as it was originally published. Not only the ending was changed — the death of the heroine replaced by a happy marriage — but the whole book was rewritten. These changes destroyed the last spark of life in the work. That which had excused all its faults was the vital spirit of a young genius just awakening in the world and tremulously unfolding its wings in a strange atmosphere. All this animation was lost, as might be expected, in the late revision. Appropriately, Louisa omitted the quotation from Emerson from which she had taken the title and which had graced the former title-page. *Moods* was no longer the same book. Louisa seems to have found, by some sort of arrangement with her conscience, an excuse for her new volume in the alterations her first publisher had required her to make. But instead of taking the occasion to revive the story in its pristine form, as logic required her to do, she took another and a longer step on the downward path.

Her very last short stories were curiously excellent. Collected in *A Garland for Girls* they show the rare quality she had of keeping in touch with contemporary life. Most of the time while these stories for adolescent girls were being written she was isolated in a sick-room and often confined to a sick-bed. Not only do they give no hint of failing spirits; they also express a vigorous sense of the life of her times. Her feeling for America in the making had come to be something almost clairvoyant.

6

Greatest of all the Alcott talents, of course, was Louisa's. The ability which distinguished her beyond all the others was the ability to tell a story. Someone with true inspiration called her a new Scheherezade. She was a born story-teller, writing tales long before she had humour, or emotion, or originality. All these things came to her with maturity. But her very earliest inventions had the essentials of illusion and excitement. She shared the story-teller's instinct possessed by the great *raconteurs* like Boccaccio, Dumas, and Dickens.

Where Louisa Alcott rose far above Bronson Alcott in greatness was in being a self-conscious artist. Louisa's father was a person of the most extraordinary but diffuse creativeness. His dreams were never focused or brought under control. Something gave Louisa the power to do this, something that she called her " brains," a resource in which she consciously put her trust. " Perhaps it isn't quite true," said Heywood Broun on one occasion, " that all great story-tellers have been persons of a low order of intelligence. I hear that Shakespeare was quite smart. But on the whole, popular tales are composed by those who believe everything they see and hear." Though not quite Shakespeare, Louisa Alcott was also smart. Consider the extremely limited experience and material on which she based her numerous and vivid stories. Of what else could she have spun the ever-widening and expanding web of her sagas but of an inward cortical secretion? Story-tellers as a rule have but a limited experience and for that reason most of them after a throw or two give up the game. It takes intelligence to spin, re-spin, and once again spin the plot. Louisa's naïve bestowal of " brains " upon herself was well justified by the vitality of her story-telling impulse. It survived in her to the very last breath of life.

Her ability to spin plots was accompanied by her ability to hold a point of view. Louisa Alcott was not of those who believe everything they see and hear. Beyond her limited Boston and Concord horizon she saw America whole. She must have done so to be the favourite author of an expanding age. In this respect like the imperialist Kipling, she was not like him in being unable to see her country's faults. The reforms she proposed were simple, for she was after all a domestic and not a market-place observer. But she was never taken in by the shams of a commercial and prosperous empire.

Few American critics and historians of literature have paid much attention to Louisa May Alcott's work. A writer for children and young readers, she seemed to them to fall outside the strictly literary category. The realization of this brought much bitterness to Louisa's last years. After Henry James her books were not seriously reviewed by the periodicals. Twenty years after her death Thomas Wentworth Higginson, the authority on so many New England authors, was quite sure that her fame would not last. " She delineated admirably the best type of plain, loving, affectionate, intelligent American families," he said. " But," he added, " for permanent fame, there must be a certain quality of art." Therefore, Mr. Higginson complacently predicted, Louisa Alcott's name would soon follow those of other forgotten authors into oblivion. After Mr. Higginson's death Gamaliel Bradford took great pains to batter down Louisa Alcott's reputation. She was, in this critic's opinion, mercenary, erratic, cold in her affections, and didactic. To these harsh strictures he added the further accusation that her work was not original. Can this eccentric charge mean that Louisa Alcott plagiarized the Alcott family history? If so, what could then be looked upon as original in fiction? Louisa Alcott's originality lies beyond the range of any eccentric definition. It is her most characteristic and most unassailable quality, the key to her great popularity.

No less unsparing a critic of Louisa is Mrs. Katharine Fullerton Gerould. " The whole tissue of the March girls' lives," says Mrs. Gerould, " is a very commonplace fabric. You know that their furniture was bad, that the simplicity of their meals, their household service, their dress, their every day manners (in spite of the myth about Amy) was simplicity of the common, not of the intelligent kind. You really would not want to spend a week in the house of any of them." This tone of criticism is a marked tribute to the reality of Louisa Alcott's stories. Someone is so affected by the life of the March girls, who are purely creatures of Louisa's imagination, that she pricks forth like Don Quixote, if not with sword, at least with pen, to destroy them. Her iconoclasm is a testimonial to greatness.

Louisa Alcott's greatness is in a peculiar field, youth, and is beyond idle questioning. The weakness of critics like the above is that they do not understand the importance of her field. This is well set forth by Frank P. Stearns, who wrote the most real and interesting sketch of Louisa Alcott in existence and who says in it: " Youth is a period of life which deserves much more consideration than it often receives. It is the integrating period, during which we make our characters and form those habits of thought and action which mainly determine our destiny. The bloom of youth may conceal this internal conflict, but it is there none the less, and frequently a very severe one. ' You have no idea how many trials I have,' I once heard a school-girl of sixteen say, the perfect picture of health and happiness; and those who remember well their own youth will not be inclined to laugh at this. The tragedy of childhood is the commonest form of tragedy; and youth is a melo-

drama in which pathos and humour are equally mingled. Those who by some chance have escaped this experience and have had the path of early life made
smooth for them, may grow to be thrifty trees but are
not likely to bear much fruit. It is for her clear perception of these conditions and her skill and address in
dealing with them that Miss Alcott deserves the celebrity that is now attached to her name."

If this is true, and perhaps it is even more true than
Frank P. Stearns and most of us realize, Louisa Alcott
devoted her life to the discovery and reporting of a
valuable continent. She was, as she would so much have
liked to be, essentially like Christopher Columbus, a
great voyager who visited an undiscovered land and
came back and told the rest of the world about it. No
one has ever since quite duplicated their achievements.

7

The long illness of Bronson Alcott was nearing its
end. At first it had but disabled him, the octogenarian
who aged peacefully among his books and newspapers
and came annually like a shadow of his former self to
the summer school at Concord. But his final failure was
very rapid. After nearly six years of enfeeblement he
suddenly lost his last weak hold on life. A month of
unconsciousness ended in his death on March 4, 1888.

In the meantime Louisa's health, never of the best,
had taken a definite turn for the worse. The strain of
her father's illness had told severely upon her, but she

had kept up a reasonable amount of activity and socia-
bility until 1886. Some vital physical resources must
have failed her about this time — some inward loss of
vitality incidental to her years. Her illness grew much
more serious. It was at this critical time that she went
into retirement at Dunreath Place in Roxbury. The
solitude of her life there may or may not have been the
best thing for her state. Her physical decline must have
been hastened by the dead weight of mental depression
which there settled upon her. Could any warm friendly
human touch have reached her, aside from her doctor's
devotion, it might have saved her life by lifting for an
instant the deep shadow which fell on her from Louisburg Square. But in her solitude no such influence
came.

Few people knew how critical was her condition. It
was generally reported in Boston that Louisa Alcott was
suffering from a prolonged case of nervous prostration.
She was actually wasting away from sleeplessness and
starving to death. Her treatment at Dunreath Place
consisted in trying to give her rest and food. The
sleeplessness yielded at last to baths and massage; but
the inability to take food steadily increased. The old
bullying family physician had said to her mercilessly:
" Eat or die! " The gentler treatment of Dunreath
Place consisted in placing constantly before her the
most tempting and dainty repasts. But nothing helped
to relieve the piteous rejection of all food which was the
only response of her ailing system. Her tall frame grew

more and more tragically emaciated and feeble. Louisa saw and felt this terrible wasting away, but she could do nothing about it.

The last sparse pages of her diary were never published; their few entries were too melancholy to bear the light. Instead, some cheerful chatty notes addressed to her Aunt Bond were disclosed. Their affected cheeriness — always her note with Aunt Bond — give small indication of the profound hopelessness which darkened her last days and found nowhere relief.

On the last day of her father's life she went to pay him her weekly visit. Each visit she paid now was a farewell. On this day, March 4, 1888, a bleak wind was blowing. As Louisa left his room to go out of the house, a caller appeared at the front door. Her sensitiveness to seeing strangers had grown so great that she darted out of a side door, and in her haste she left her fur wrap lying in the hall. She was not quick enough, however, to escape the glance of the caller who entered. The impression Louisa made on the visitor is our last objective glimpse of her. So wasted and fragile had she grown, says Miss Porter, in the interval since she had last seen her that she realized in an instant that Louisa was very dangerously ill. This was not the general attitude of Boston. Her death came to everyone as a great shock.

Emerging into the bleak, wind-swept square, Louisa hurried into her carriage and was driven to Roxbury. The drive without her wrap brought too much exposure for her under-nourished state. She arrived with a chill and was immediately put to bed. While they tended her, Bronson Alcott died. It must be that they regarded his daughter already as a very sick woman, for she was not told that day of his death. The next morning she awoke with a severe headache — so severe that other doctors beside Dr. Lawrence were summoned. Her frame had no resistance to disease of any kind. What developed was described as spinal meningitis and also as an apoplectic stroke; the disease came so quickly that no one knew exactly what it was. It seemed almost as if her exhausted life, in the phrase of Anatole France, consented to cease.

After her illness began, she quickly lapsed into an unconscious state. From this she emerged only to recognize her adopted nephew and Dr. Rhoda Lawrence. Her surviving sister, Mrs. Anna Pratt, having finished at last her long, long care of their aged father, went out to Roxbury to her bedside. But Louisa did not recognize the playmate of her childhood. The next day, March 6, 1888, she was still no better; and in the afternoon, at the hour of her father's funeral ceremony, she died. She had to the last never known of her father's death.

Very appropriately Louisa Alcott was buried by young people. Her two nephews and a young sculptor friend took charge of the funeral, conveying the body from Roxbury first to Louisburg Square and thence by train to Concord. It was taken to Sleepy Hollow and placed in a grave beside her father's. Young hands covered both graves simultaneously with palms and laurel wreaths. The ceremony recalls the day so many years before this when Louisa and her father were crowned by children's hands with wreaths in honour of their common birthday. Always since then they had celebrated their birthday together. They had come together to that last and final celebration of their earthly existence.

Near the spot where they laid Louisa Alcott was the grave of the author of *The Scarlet Letter*. Not far from her slept the author of *The American Scholar*. Adjacent to her rested the great inspiration of the transcendental movement — her father. As the author of *Little Women* was added to the company, falling clods tolled the end of a great American era. Louisa May Alcott was its last representative.

BIBLIOGRAPHY

BARTLETT, TRUMAN A.: *The Art Life of Wm. Rimmer, Sculptor*. Boston: Jas. R. Osgood and Co.; 1882.

BATES, E. S., and DITTEMORE, J. V.: *Mary Baker Eddy: The Truth and the Tradition*. New York: Alfred A. Knopf; 1932.

BOLTON, SARAH K.: *Lives of Girls Who Became Famous*. New York: T. Y. Crowell Co.; 1925.

BONSTELLE, JESSIE, and DE FOREST, MARIAN: *Little Women Letters from the House of Alcott*. Boston: Little, Brown and Co.; 1914.

BRADFORD, GAMALIEL: *Portraits of American Women*. Boston: Houghton, Mifflin Co.; 1917.

BROWN, MARY HOSMER: *Memories of Concord*. Boston: The Four Seas Co.; 1926.

CAIRNS, C. C.: *A Book of Noble Women*. London: T. C. and E. C. Jack; 1923.

CATHER, KATHERINE DUNLAP: *Younger Days of Famous Writers*. New York: Century Co.; 1925.

CHENEY, EDNAH D. editor: *Louisa May Alcott. Her Life, Letters, and Journals*. Boston: Little, Brown and Co.; 1928.

CHENEY, EDNAH D.: *Reminiscences*. Boston: Lee and Shepherd; 1902.

CLARK, ANNIE M. L.: *The Alcotts in Harvard*. Lancaster, Mass.: J. C. L. Clark; 1902.

GEROULD, KATHARINE FULLERTON: *Modes and Morals*. New York: Charles Scribner's Sons; 1920.

GOWING, CLARA: *The Alcotts As I Knew Them*. Boston: C. M. Clark; 1909.

GRISWOLD, HATTIE TYNG: *Sketches of Recent Authors*. Chicago: McClurg; 1898.

GULLIVER, LUCILE: *Louisa May Alcott: A Bibliography*. Boston: Little, Brown and Co.; 1932.

HARLOW, LURABEL: *Louisa May Alcott: A Souvenir.* Boston: Sam'l E. Cassino; 1888.

HAWTHORNE, JULIAN: *Nathaniel Hawthorne and His Wife.* Boston: Jas. R. Osgood and Co.; 1885.

HIGGINSON, T. W.: *Short Studies of American Authors.* New York: Longmans, Green and Co.; 1906.

HOWE, M. A. DE W.: *Memories of a Hostess. The Diaries of Mrs. Jas. T. Fields.* Boston: Little, Brown and Co.; 1922.

JAMES, HENRY: *Daisy Miller.* New York: Harper and Brothers; 1878.

JAMES, HENRY: *Hawthorne.* New York: Harper and Brothers; 1880.

JAMES, HENRY: *Notes and Reviews.* Cambridge, Mass.: Dunster House, 1921.

LANE, CHARLES: *The Law and Method in Spirit Culture. An Interpretation of A. Bronson Alcott's Idea and Practice in the Masonic Temple.* Boston: Jas. Munroe and Co.; 1843.

MARTINEAU, HARRIET: *Society in America.* New York: Saunders and Otley; 1837.

MEIGS, CORNELIA: *Invincible Louisa.* Boston: Little, Brown and Co.; 1933.

Morgan Library MSS. Collection. Papers read at the John Brown Memorial Meeting, December 2, 1859, by Emerson, Thoreau, Alcott and others.

MORROW, HONORÉ WILLSIE: *Father of Little Women.* Boston: Little, Brown and Co.; 1927.

MOSES, BELLE: *Louisa May Alcott: Dreamer and Worker.* New York: D. Appleton and Co.; 1923.

MOULTON, LOUISA CHANDLER: *Our Famous Women.* Hartford, Conn.: Worthington; 1884.

RAYMOND, CHARLES HARLOW: *Story Lives of Master Writers.* New York: F. A. Stokes Co.; 1927.

REED, MYRTLE: *Happy Women.* New York: G. P. Putnam's Sons; 1913.

ROBINSON, H. J. H.: *Massachusetts in the Woman Suffrage Movement.* Boston: Roberts Brothers; 1881.

BIBLIOGRAPHY

SANBORN, F. B.: *Recollections of Seventy Years*. Boston: Richard Badger; 1909.

SANBORN, F. B., and HARRIS, W. T.: *A. Bronson Alcott: His Life and Philosophy*. Boston: Roberts Brothers; 1893.

SEARS, CLARA E.: *Bronson Alcott's Fruitlands*. Boston: Houghton Mifflin Co.; 1915.

STANTON, E. C., and ANTHONY, SUSAN B.: *History of Woman Suffrage*. Rochester, N. Y.; 1881–.

STEARNS, FRANK P.: *Sketches from Concord*. New York: G. P. Putnam's Sons; 1895.

TICKNOR, CAROLINE: *May Alcott: A Memoir*. Boston: Little, Brown and Co.; 1928.

WHITING, LILIAN: *Women Who Have Ennobled Life*. Philadelphia: The Union Press; 1915.

WILLIAMS, SHERMAN: *Some Successful Americans*. Boston: Ginn and Co.; 1904.

WILLIS, FREDERICK L. H.: *Alcott Memoirs*. Boston: Richard Badger; 1915.

MAGAZINE ARTICLES

ALCOTT, JOHN S. P.: "Little Women of Long Ago." *Good Housekeeping*, February 1913.

ASHMUN, MARGARET: "On a Portrait of Miss Alcott." Poem. *New England Magazine*, September 1907.

BEER, THOMAS: "An Irritating Archangel." *The Bookman*, December 1927.

HILLYER, LAURIE: "Abigail May Alcott." *Parents' Magazine*, November 1932.

JAMES, HENRY: "Eight Cousins, or the Aunt Hill." Review. *The Nation*, October 14, 1875.

PORTER, MARIA S.: "Recollections of Louisa May Alcott." *New England Magazine*, March 1892.

SANBORN, F. B.: "Reminiscences of Louisa M. Alcott." *Independent*, March 1912.

SPOFFORD, HARRIET PRESCOTT: "Louisa May Alcott." *The Chautauquan,* December 1888.

"When Alcott Books Were New." *Publishers' Weekly,* September 28, 1931.

WHITMAN, ALFRED: "Miss Alcott's Letters to Her Laurie." *Ladies' Home Journal,* October 1901.

WOOD, LYDIA HOSMER: "Beth Alcott's Playmate." *Harper's Bazaar,* May 1913.

WRITINGS OF THE ALCOTT FAMILY

The Writings of Louisa May Alcott:

Flower Fables. Boston: Geo. W. Briggs and Co.; 1855.

"Thoreau's Flute." Poem. *The Atlantic,* May 1863.

Hospital Sketches. Boston: Redpath; 1863.

Moods. Boston: A. K. Loring; 1865.

Little Women: or Meg, Jo, Beth, and Amy. Boston: Roberts Brothers; Part I, 1868; Part II, 1869.

Camp and Fireside Stories (with Hospital Sketches). Boston: Roberts Brothers; 1869.

An Old-Fashioned Girl. Boston: Roberts Brothers; 1870.

Little Men: Life at Plumfield with Jo's Boys. Boston: Roberts Brothers; 1871.

Aunt Jo's Scrap Bag. Boston: Roberts Brothers.

   My Boys. 1872.

   Shawl-Straps. 1872.

   Cupid and Chow-Chow. 1874.

   My Girls. 1878.

   Jimmy's Cruise in the Pinafore. 1879.

   An Old-Fashioned Thanksgiving. 1882.

Work: A Story of Experience. Boston: Roberts Brothers; 1873.

Eight Cousins: or the Aunt-Hill. Boston: Roberts Brothers; 1875.

Silver Pitchers. Boston: Roberts Brothers; 1876.

Rose in Bloom. A Sequel to "Eight Cousins." Boston: Roberts Brothers; 1876.

A Modern Mephistopheles. Boston: Roberts Brothers; 1877.

Under the Lilacs. Boston: Roberts Brothers; 1878.

Jack and Jill. Boston: Roberts Brothers; 1880.

Proverb Stories. Boston: Roberts Brothers; 1882.

Moods. Boston: Roberts Brothers; 1882.

Spinning-Wheel Stories. Boston: Roberts Brothers; 1884.

Jo's Boys, and How They Turned Out. A Sequel to "Little Men." Boston: Roberts Brothers; 1886.

Lulu's Library. Boston: Roberts Brothers; Volume I, 1886; Volume II, 1887; Volume III, 1889.

A Garland for Girls. Boston: Roberts Brothers; 1888.

Three Unpublished Poems. Boston: Clara E. Sears; 1919.

" M. L." Journal of Negro History, October 1929.

The principal works in the foregoing list are translated and read in the following foreign countries: Great Britain, Norway, Sweden, Denmark, Finland, The Netherlands, France, Germany, Austria, Italy, Poland, Hungary, Czechoslovakia, Russia, Spain, Portugal, Japan.

The Writings of A. Bronson Alcott:

Observations on the Principles and Methods of Infant Instruction. Boston: Carter and Hendee; 1830.

Conversations on the Gospels. Boston: James Munroe and Co., 1837.

Concord Days. Boston: Roberts Brothers; 1872.

(And E. P. Peabody) *Record of a School, Exemplifying the Principles and Methods of Moral Culture.* Boston: Roberts Brothers; 1874.

Table Talk. Boston: Roberts Brothers; 1877.

Tablets. Boston: Roberts Brothers; 1879.

Sonnets and Canzonets. Boston: Roberts Brothers; 1882.

New Connecticut: An Autobiography. Boston: Roberts Brothers; 1887.

By Louisa M. Alcott and Anna B. Pratt:

Comic Tragedies. Written by " Jo" and "Meg" and acted by the Little Women. Boston: Roberts Brothers; 1893.

By May Alcott Nieriker:

Concord Sketches. Consisting of Twelve Original Drawings by May Alcott. Boston: Fields, Osgood and Co.; 1869.

Studying Art Abroad and How to Do It Cheaply. Boston: Roberts Brothers; 1879.

Index